Death in the Irish Sea

The Sinking of the
RMS Leinster

Roy Stokes

THE COLLINS PRESS

First published in 1998 by
The Collins Press, West Link Park, Doughcloyne,
Wilton, Cork.
© Roy Stokes 1998

This publication has received support from the Heritage Council under the 1998
Publications Grant Scheme

British Library cataloguing in publication data.

A CIP catalogue record for this book is avaiable
from the British Library.

Printed in Ireland by Sci Print, Shannon.

Designed by Stephanie J Dagg, Virtually Perfect Editing Services.
Jacket design by Upper Case Ltd, Cork.
ISBN: 1-898256-52-7

Dedication

There has been a great tussle in my mind as to whom I should dedicate this book.

I would like to dedicate this book to the memory of merchant seamen who died at sea during World War One and the 9,000,000 others who never returned from a horrific episode in our history.

However, on 26 July, 1997 I lost a friend in the person of Frank Price who died while we were diving on the wreck. He was a remarkable, kind and humorous man who will always be missed. I know now that to whom the dedication is made does not really matter, because we have lost him, but these lovely words by the poet Alfred Lord Tennyson may somehow help his family, friends and I to soothe his passing.

Crossing the bar

Sunset and evening star,
And one clear call for me!
And may there be no moaning of the bar,
When I put to sea.

But such a tide as moving seems asleep,
Too full for sound and foam,
When that which drew from out the boundless deep
Turns again home.

Twilight and evening bell,
And after that the dark!
And may there be no sadness of farewell,
When I embark;

For tho' from out our bourne of Time and Place
The flood may bear me far,
I hope to see my Pilot face
When I have crost the bar.

Acknowledgements

I wish to give special thanks to the following for their constant encouragement and assistance with research material: Edward Burke for persistent encouragement; Des Brannigan for access to the wreck and research material; C. Louth for excellent corrections and suggestions; Noel Brian for suggestions and research material; Kevin Crothers for unwavering support and my apologies to anyone I have accidentally omitted.

And last but not least my wife and partner Ann.

Contents

Introduction

The sinking of the Royal Mail Steamer *Leinster*, a short distance from Dublin Bay in an operational area known as 'Square-72', occurred during a period when events in Ireland and throughout the world were climaxing with the end to a terrible conflict.

The Irish Rebellion was two years old and Home Rule was in the balance. The end of the First World War was imminent, yet the German submarine fleet was still desperately trying to salvage some honour by continuing savage assaults on shipping.

The conscription of Irish citizens had been threatened almost daily, and in an effort to defeat the advancing German Army and Navy, that giant of a nation - the USA - finally joined hands across the water with their Allies in 1917. This joint effort against a common enemy forged new European-American friendships which survive to this day.

It is also the account of a government's reckless abandonment in its refusal to protect the travelling public and a commercial shipping company's vessels at a time when it could easily have done so.

The sinking of the *Leinster* remains to this day the greatest disaster to befall Irish citizens travelling in Irish waters. This remarkable episode, although remembered from time to time on various maritime occasions, has not received the recognition due to it. Only very recently did the owner of the *Leinster's* remains, Desmond Brannigan, and several subaqua divers from the locality of Dun Laoghaire harbour rectify this lapse of memory. With financial assistance from Stena Sealink, Irish Lights and others later mentioned, they raised one of the wreck's anchors. Mounted opposite the Carlisle Pier, it is a fitting reminder of the many local people who served and travelled aboard the mail steamers and, in particular, to the 500 or more who lost their lives while travelling on the *Leinster*.

The violence and the unusually high death toll associated with this tragedy is still not comprehended and is in dark contrast with the many pleasant and tranquil Victorian depictions of the Mail Boats exhibited throughout Dun Laoghaire's hotels, pubs and banks.

With only a few short weeks before Germany and England ended hostilities, men and women continued to be recruited for war. With thousands still to die, Ireland, and in particular the city of Dublin, was a place that remained generally 'removed' from the hostilities of the Great War and was an itch that many leading figures just could not scratch. Ireland was seen as being in just as much danger from the onslaught of German aggressive expansionism but was somehow specially exempt from full commitment to Europe's defence and ultimately its own. The chief censor at The Admiralty, Rear Admiral Sir Douglas Browning, encapsulated this attitude in a passage contained in his recollections that he published in 1920. Whilst visiting Admiralty wireless stations in March 1916, he had occasion to stop over in Sligo with a burst tyre where he made a visit to the 'cinema house or barn ... After climbing many stairs I joined the local "knuts" to see a fine show'. Faced with the shock notice on the screen proclaiming the final chapter would be shown 'next week', he wondered 'if the locals felt the same or

1

were they inured to cinema shocks, as they were the only shocks to which Ireland was exposed during the war!'

Ireland was a country whose conscience was in conflict. On the one hand, it despised the British occupation, but on the other, many who were not fighting in foreign parts in defence of the Realm could be found working all the hours God could send, fitting and repairing the British Fleet, producing munitions and generally supporting the War Effort.

Although submarine attacks in the Irish Sea were not unheard of, their casualties were generally perceived to be small. This complacency within Ireland was shattered when it received the unbelievable news of the sinking of the mail boat *Leinster* by a German submarine on 10 October, 1918. When the bodies began to come ashore, Ireland gasped at the scale of the disaster that was revealed. To many it came as a complete surprise, but to the seamen on the route and the Ministry Of Defence, it had been inevitable. Indeed, it had been almost a miracle that these mail steamers had escaped until then. The protection of the mail boats was the responsibility of Flag Captain Gordon Campbell VC who commanded the Irish Sea Flotilla and, although not his only worry, he expressed the view that the loss of a mail steamer 'would be considered a national disaster'.

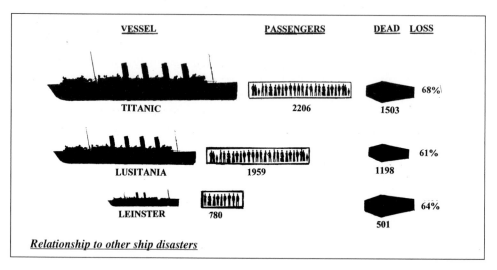

Relationship to other ship disasters

Censorship of the press was total, so the clarion cries of 'Murdering Hun', were commonplace as before, with the only one small exception of an attempted 'Stop Press' edition by the *Evening Herald* on 10 October. The justification for this attack, and the knowledge of several previous ones, was suppressed in order to temper public reaction during a recruiting drive that was about to go into full swing. Many argue that the use of censorship and propaganda are a necessary part of a War. This, I believe to be true during 1914-1918, and a small price to pay if you consider that munitions production, troop movements, ability of equipment etc., if kept secret, may ultimately have saved lives and shortened the war. However, in the context of the 'Irish Question' and that of the *'Leinster* Affair'and its immediate aftermath, it would seem to me that this power was abused and civilian life was unnecessarily put at risk.

The loss of the *Leinster* also marked the demise of its owners, the City of Dublin Steam Packet Co., which had been in the steam packet business since 1823. This ship was the second in its quartet of famous mail steamers to be lost in the War and was the final nail in a coffin that made trading unsustainable. Despite extremely difficult and sometimes discriminatory operating parameters, this company produced excellent vessels that served Dublin and the cross-channel ferry service well. Shortly after the end of the War, and probably because of it, this company which had pioneered technical innovations in all of its vessels and upheld the highest standards in a very popular service, faded into obscurity.

Although in relative terms, this tragedy was far greater than that of the much publicised *Titanic* and *Lusitania*, it has received comparatively little publicity. The following chapters are an attempt to redress this and, in so doing, highlight the roll and the activities of these mail boat ferries on the Irish Sea. It also sets out to make clear the enormity of the event, and to pay tribute to those brave and wonderful unsung heroes who effected a rescue on that early morning.

This account also includes a short history of the City of Dublin Steam Packet Co. (CDSPCo.) extending into the outbreak of the First World War. By extracting data from various sources, I have attempted to demonstrate the enormous scale to which the U-boat campaign affected the Admiralty and Ireland and how extensive these U-boat patrols were in the Irish Sea during the closing months of the War. I also address some of the issues of the War years which were clouded by Ireland's own 'troubles' and finally climaxed during the controversy surrounding 'The *Leinster* Affair'.

As there are many brilliant accounts of this period, this story, although relying on such works, is not intended to be a history of the War, but an extractive account of those relevant situations and circumstances surrounding the loss of the *Leinster*.

We are tempted to remember this War in terms of our grandparents and the stories they passed on to us as children. But they were the survivors. Those who died in terrible conditions in godforsaken places were no more than boys and they were killed in their millions.

Chapter 1
The precipice

When the winter of 1916 arrived, Britain and her Allies had been at war with Germany for over two years. Despite sacrificing millions of lives, and with vast lands of Europe laid waste, neither side could dominate the other into submission. One of the main strategies adopted by both sides was a sea blockade. For the Allies, it meant physical barriers across the North sea, the English Channel, entrances to the Irish sea and into the Mediterranean. This method included the use of armed merchantmen, nets, mines and a multitude of all manner of craft, including aircraft. Early expectations from these enormous operations had been well overestimated and at best could only have been considered merely a 'stop gap' intervention. In the North Atlantic, the North Sea and the English Channel, the blockading fleets did manage to reduce the flow of shipping and supplies to Germany.

Germany attempted the task with a totally different method. Following the declaration by Germany in February 1915 to include the waters around Ireland within the 'War Zone', it deployed its growing U-boat fleet into the Atlantic Approaches and beyond the Allied blockade. This had the effect of not only harassing locally dispersed shipping and approaching convoys, but also carrying attacks on shipping to the doorstep of the United States of America. The effects of the submarine war were both crippling and unexpected. The situation quickly approached a crisis of unthinkable proportions.

Although both sides had maintained quite large and roughly equal 'on sea' battle fleets, they rarely engaged on a grand scale. The very fact that one fleet existed gave rise to the necessity for the maintenance and ability to deploy the other. This negative dependence was accentuated to the extreme with '100' valuable destroyers tied up babysitting the British Grand Fleet. This was at a time when German submarines were threatening the very existence of Britain because of the absence of these destroyers for escort duties and submarine hunting. So for this aspect of the War, little was decided. Beneath the sea was quite another matter.

After a hesitant beginning, Germany's submarine development streaked ahead that of the Allies. Still a relatively new concept, Germany seized it and, aided by the development by Krupps of a powerful and reliable diesel powered engine, surpassed anything the Allies had in quality and production techniques. The mastery of U-boat development aided an even more sinister development by Germany. This was the use of submarines to deploy mines. Mine laying by the Germans around Ireland was at first kept secret by the British as the implications were frightening. It had taken the Admiralty completely by surprise when the brand new 23,000 ton battleship *Audacious* was sunk by a mine off Lough Swilly in 1914. The prospect that overtook the Admiralty was that if allowed to continue, the British Isles could have become awash with these threatening 'black eggs of destruction', thus threatening the merchant marine with confinement.

As far back as January 1915, and for the first time, a German submarine marauded up the Irish Sea, presenting the Admiralty with the obvious and shocking possibilities. By then the Germans were well situated to advance and develop submarine warfare, which they accomplished at frightening speed. It had become clear that the Western approaches were actually the highways to Britain by which it maintained its peoples. If the situation had been allowed to continue unchecked and without innovation, the approaches to the British Isles would soon have been choked by German submarines. Not since Napoleon had a foreign power threatened Britain in its own waters.

When 1917 arrived, disaster heaped upon disaster, forcing the Allies to reconsider the course of the war. There was the massive squandering of human life at The Somme, Verdun and also at The Dardanelles, where German and English submarines began to play a more aggressive and decisive role. Before spring arrived, allied forces on the West and Eastern Fronts were in open revolt. In the case of the East, this precipitated the fall of the Tsar of Russia, the return of Lenin and the Great Bolshevik Revolution. The war was not going well for the Allies and, worse still, there was no prospect that the situation would improve. And there was the growing and inescapable inevitability of the 'German U-boat Threat'.

The difficulties in counteracting the growing 'U-boat Menace' had been overwhelming. Resources available to the British Admiralty were stretched thin about the globe and this forced the application of a wide variety of vessels and methods. These included armed pleasure yachts, fishing vessels, paddle steamers, armed merchantmen, miles of wire nets, mines and, of course, the Admiralty's powerful but overstretched and dwindling warships. In an effort to assist the Admiralty, a number of air bases were commissioned around the British Isles, including several in Ireland. These were initially operated by the RAF, the RNAS and later augmented by the United States Navy. Here again there was a variety of craft in use, but in the Irish theatre of operations, they were confined mainly to airships and seaplanes.

For the duration of the War, the Western Approaches were patrolled and commanded from Queenstown, County Cork. Although picturesque, this base at the outbreak of the War had the reputation of being an under-equipped and sleepy little backwater. It was not considered a desirable posting, especially for an officer who might seek rapid promotion. This perception of Queenstown later disappeared and many officers who served there became very prominent in their careers.

Shocked by the rapid advances of the German submarines and their ability to bring the War to the doorstep of any one of Britain's major ports, the Admiralty made a series of what can only be effectively described as 'better than gestures'. Barrages of fishing vessels trawling wire nets were situated throughout European waters in such places as the Dover Straits, between Milfordhaven and Ireland and between Larne and Scotland. Hoping desperately to encourage fishermen and merchant seamen to keep a weather eye open for U-boats, various rewards or 'prizes' were made for sightings and sinkings. One such scheme was the Sir Alfred F. Yarrow Award which promised £20 for the reported sighting of a U-boat. This situation would seem to lend itself to far more sightings than there were actual submarines if it had not been for the fact that the sighting had to be officially confirmed. If you were lucky enough to sink a U-boat, your ship could receive as much as £1,000, topped up further by a salvage award if the vessel was captured. This was no modest amount at that time.

There were literally thousands of vessels employed, but suffering severely from a lack of valuable and more suitable warships, only a modest measure of effect was achieved. Their actual accomplishment was to somewhat hamper the movements of the submarines but did nothing to improve the ability to sink them. The German U-boat commanders were by then equal to the advanced vessels with which they were being supplied. In increasing numbers they attacked shipping right around the British Isles. They had the edge, and it became their intention to strangle the sea lanes to Britain.

The command at Queenstown had been relieved a little in 1916 when a number of Royal Navy 'Flower Class' sloops were delivered. These vessels had a top speed that could more than match the maximum fifteen knots of the German submarines. They were well armed and cleverly designed vessel, and whilst initially deployed on Ireland's South coast, they covered an operational area of as much as 1,500 square miles each. (These areas were reduced to as little as thirty square miles in places towards the end of the war.) But alas, Admiral Bayly of Queenstown Command would have been happier with 'another twenty'. Figuring increasingly were the Admiralty's fast P boats and motor launches (MLs) which were supplied by the United States in increasing numbers. These were surprising boats that were assembled in the USA. The main feature of these lightly built, eighty foot boats was their ability to operate at high speeds, even in rough weather. When flat out, they could reach speeds of up to thirty knots, but they could not sustain this without serious risk to machinery.

Prior to the War, the USA had been pioneering the use of motor torpedo boats (MTBs), at a time during which a young commander was to gain prominence. Graduating from the Naval Academy in Florida in 1890 and specialising in engineering, he began a long and illustrious career. In 1907, Commander H.I. Cone sailed a flotilla of similar type vessels from the East coast of the USA, through the Magellan Straits and up the West coast to San Francisco. For his achievement he was commended by President T. Roosevelt; he would later receive many additional commendations. As a commander, he saw extensive and world wide service and was in the forefront of the development of the MTB. Devoted to his career, he later commanded the US Naval Aviation Forces Foreign Services from London in September 1917. It was whilst he was headquartered there that he figured bravely in the *Leinster* tragedy.

A most interesting method employed by the Admiralty to sink German submarines was the use of 'Q' ships, or as they became known, 'Mystery Ships'. The broad strategy was to lure enemy U-boats into thinking that what they saw through the periscope was a vulnerable merchantman. But when the enemy surfaced (wherever possible and especially earlier in the war, in order to conserve torpedoes, U-boats preferred to sink ships by gunfire or by placing explosives in the ship's hold), the 'innocent merchantman' revealed cleverly concealed heavy weaponry and commenced firing on the startled enemy. This type of engagement became nail-biting stuff, as quite often the German submarine would get first 'crack'. As a result of long periods of cruising and awaiting attack, the tension often led to breakdown and fatigue amongst the crews.

In this theatre there were several controversial incidents, such as the infamous 'Baralong Affair' off the South coast of Ireland in 1915. In this, the British

Baralong mystery ship was said to have been flying a US flag when it came on the unsuspecting U-27. The German U-boat had apprehended the freighter *Nicosian* and, while on the blind side, was surprised by the *Baralong*. Not one of the German submariners escaped slaughter, either aboard their submarine or struggling in the water, nor in the *Nicosian* into which some of them were chased. Hoping to escape the raking gunfire from the *Baralong*, they hid in the engine room, where a boarding party eventually located and killed them in a most horrible manner. This was said to be a revenge killing for the *Lusitania* and *Arabic* incidents.

Conversion of these mystery steamers was extensive - from fittings to funnels, from uniforms to guns. They were completed in many shipyards, not least of which Hawlboline at Queenstown gained something of a reputation. It was while the celebrated Gordon Campbell VC was in command of the 'Q' ship Pargust that it sunk *UC-29* off the South coast of Ireland. This action resulted in a number of awards and distinctions being handed down to the crew, including two VCs. Gordon Campbell received an extra Bar and quick promotion to captain. Captain Campbell was particularly successful with this method against U-boats, knocking out three before he was promoted to command the Irish Sea Flotilla in 1918.

Despite its strong currents, and because of its narrowness, the Dover Strait did not present any logistical problem for blockading. But the notion of trying to prevent merchant shipping crossing the North Atlantic to German or Scandinavian ports was quite a different prospect. Patrols of armed and converted merchantmen were established from the Northern shores of Scotland to as far north as Iceland and as far east as Norway. Their purpose was to stop and board vessels and prevent any type of contraband or suspicious cargoes from reaching Germany. These patrols operated in the most difficult weather conditions but eventually overcame many hardships and achieved the status of an extremely effective fleet of block-aders. Up until late 1916 these patrols operated under the umbrella of the '10th Cruiser Squadron'. They became quite an effective blockade, despite the know-ledge that many of the cargoes bound from the USA to neutral Scandinavian ports were actually continuing on to their ultimate destinations in Germany. Their efforts were also negated somewhat by the fact that they were not affecting any of the overland trade with Germany. Although these blockaders grew in effectiveness, it was the eventual acquiescence of the Scandinavian countries that put the final logistical and commercial squeeze on Germany.

Little comfort was gained from successes in blockading, as a crisis of resources was then looming. Shortages and an inability by the various ministries to replenish all manner of vessels, armaments, fuel oil, mines and so on, was exposing Britain to an inevitable and potentially disastrous outcome.

Following the declaration of an 'unrestricted U-boat campaign' and the worsening of relations between Germany and the USA in February 1917, the German U-boats began to tighten their grip in the area of the North Channel and the South Western Approaches, harassing shipping right around the coasts of Ireland. For all the effectiveness of the thousands of vessels employed by the Admiralty, they could not sink sufficient numbers of submarines or even dent the German production capability of three submarines per week. By far the Admir-alty's best vessels for the protection of shipping were her fast destroyers, P-Boats

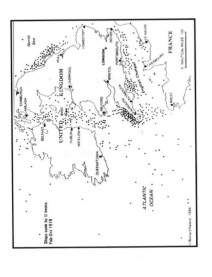

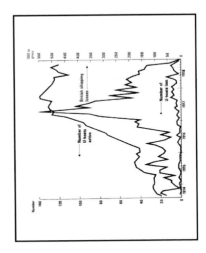

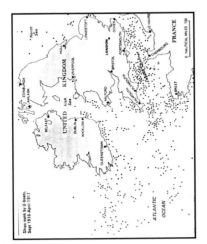

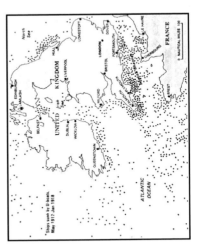

Summaries of sinking of U-boats. Of particular interest is the number of sinkings in the Irish Sea during 1918 and the desperate resurgence of U-boat activity in the latter half of 1918

and motor launches, but at that time they were not in possession of sufficient numbers for them to be deployed at their operational best.

When spring of 1917 arrived, the April figures revealed the Admiralty's worst fears. They showed a loss in excess of 600,000 tons of British shipping and nearly 1,000,000 tons globally, with the loss of only two German submarines. The June figures were even more depressing at 631,000 tons. Subsequent losses up to December of that year amounted to 2,362,000 tons. The gross accumulated loss for the year was 6,000,000 tons. It was also estimated in April that Britain's losses could reach 1,000,000 tons per month during the approaching and longer summer days. These figures may not appear excessive in terms of today's multi-thousand ton vessels, but considering that the average size of vessel then was something between a few hundred and a couple of thousand tons, this figure will be seen to represent an awful lot of ships. Not included in these figures, and of growing concern, were the increasing non-Allied losses, such as Italian, Swedish, Japanese and, of course, American vessels. The magnificent fleet of large Norwegian sailing ships suffered particularly badly in 1917 and was almost completely wiped out.

Figures not often mentioned, nor appreciated, were the loss of 178 U-boats and 5,400 of their crew who killed over 15,000 merchant seamen. Allied merchant seamen fatalities were in excess of that in any of the navies and in 1917 the effects became critical. The US Ambassador in London, Walter Page, seemed to have a grasp of the impending peril when he wrote: 'The Germans are building submarines faster than the English sink them ... The submarines are sinking freight ships faster than the freight ships are being built by the whole world ... If this goes on long enough the Allies' game is up.'

It was becoming increasingly obvious that if the devastating German U-boat attacks could not be halted, Britain would not only be starved but would also be sued for a peace that was likely to be extremely unfavourable. By Britain's own admission, it certainly looked as if it were going to lose the war - an event that could be at hand as early as November. It is also clear, since it was inevitable that it was this situation, and the earlier shrewd political calculation by the USA, that drew that country into the war at this juncture and not the loss of 'innocent American civilians', such as those who were lost on the *Lusitania* or any other US vessels that were sunk.

It has been conjectured that the USA delayed direct intervention in the war until 1917 for the following reasons:

1. That it was unnecessary to intervene as long as the commerce of the USA was not affected and that Britain was in no danger of losing the war. Cargoes, contraband or otherwise, that were running the gauntlet of the blockaders in the North Sea were by and large emanating from the USA with the full knowledge that their ultimate destination was Germany. The same was true of cargoes from other equally neutral countries.

2. That the more Germany was stretched, the easier it would be to defeat it if intervention was ultimately required. This was, in fact, the case as relatively few US servicemen were lost in the war. This is a factor of unique importance to the American public as was demonstrated during the Vietnam and Gulf wars.

3. The more Britain was stretched, the more dependant it would become on the resources of the USA and ultimately the more the USA would stand to gain. Ultimately, this reliance by Britain on the USA gave the American War Department considerable influence and control on the style of war that followed.

The earlier willingness of the USA to supply arms and material was similar to its 'cash and carry' policy adopted in the early years of the Second World War, and its delay in entering into the affray could be compared to its isolationist policy as expressed by Mr Roosevelt in 1935 when he said: 'We shun political commitments which might entangle us in foreign wars; we avoid connexion with the political activities of the League Of Nations ... We seek to isolate ourselves completely from war.'

American investment in, and recruitment for, the War got into full swing and this led to growing and disapproving glares at Ireland's 'special situation'. The Troubles in Ireland were no longer confined to just 'pig breeders' and 'spies' as we shall see later. Caught in a delicate bind of whether or not to implement conscription, and with the growing threats of the Nationalist Sinn Féiners, Britain trod cautiously. The German U-boat campaign had been responsible for unacceptably high shipping losses in 1917, but there was no doubt that the industrial might of the USA would eventually prevail and compel an end to the war.

The Irish conscience was continually and equally assaulted by both England and America with the legitimate argument that a German dictator had never, and would never, do anything to further the Irish cause. The problem Irish Nationalism had with this argument was that having suffered long and deep-rooted oppression under British rule, it was not convinced that it would benefit by the spilling of its blood in 'Defence of the Realm'. The deal was Home Rule in return for an unfettered abundance of enthusiastic Irish volunteers for the battlefields. The native suspicion was that Home Rule would not come up trumps. The threat was the introduction of conscription. Ireland's 'special situation' was not helped by what was perceived as a 'stab in the back' on 24 April 1916, when the Easter Rebellion erupted. Following the failed insurrection a 'German Plot' was uncovered in May. This once more unleashed the 'G' men from Dublin Castle who rounded up the usual disloyal suspects. The Easter Rebellion failed, not least because of the capture of the German gun-running ship *Aud off* Cork three days earlier. In it was a large consignment of arms which Roger Casement had obtained from an opportunistic German government. This conspiracy with Germany was seen not only by the British, but also by many Home Rulers, as treacherous and Roger Casement together with the leaders of the Rebellion paid for it with their lives.

Demonstrating a display of impatience with this 'special situation', the big stick was finally wielded in early April 1918 when the powers of the Conscription Act received the Royal Assent for extension to all of Ireland. Comments such as the following from the Earl of Dunraven inflamed the Nationalists further and contributed to widespread labour unrest and civil disruption: 'Ireland is full of refugees from military service. It was a funk hole for men who wished to evade service.'

THE IRISH TIMES, FRIDAY, APRIL 19, 1918.

CONSCRIPTION FOR IRELAND.

ACT RECEIVES THE ROYAL ASSENT.

LORD DUNRAVEN AND THE NATIONALISTS.

THE DUKE OF ABERCORN AND THE CONVENTION'S ATTITUDE.

From The Irish Times *of Friday 19 April 1918*

Given the vast resources of the USA, it was a secure bet that if it entered the conflict it would change the course of the war. However, not unlike the miscalculation of the Japanese a quarter of a century later, the Germans misread the Americans' intentions. They had coldly calculated the loss rates in merchant shipping to arrive at the assumption that they would conclude the war by August, thus rendering any assistance the USA might bring to be ineffective and too late.

We know now that they underestimated their new foe and almost immediately a reversal of fortunes was attained by America's insistence on the introduction of the 'convoy system'.

Although the German U-boat campaign had not only continued during 1917 but actually intensified, it was no match for the new resources and the developing strengths and skills of the Anglo-American Navy. In 1917, the new Alliance implemented several key decisions that turned the tables:

1. The introduction of a long forgotten method of protecting ships during war -the Convoy and Patrol Lane Systems.
2. The supply of many vessels from the USA and, in particular, fast patrol boats.
3. The extensive use of depth charges.
4. The introduction of barrages of mines in the Dover Strait, the Heligoland Bight and the Great North Sea Barrage.

This latter undertaking was an operation of enormous industrial enterprise and had been considered practically impossible. It consisted of a web of mines stretching 240 miles between Scotland and Norway at a cost of $40,000,000 and was probably the largest single undertaking of the War. At the insistence of the USA, this scheme involved the manufacture and transportation of huge quantities of new and advanced mines from the USA which were assembled in Scotland and provided for laying at the rate of 2,000 per day. The project was to involve the laying of up to 120,000 mines, providing an impenetrable wall right across the North Sea.

The result of all this was that during 1917-1918, German submarine losses reached an unsustainable rate of two per week. This more than negated production and eventually contributed to the demoralisation of not only submarine crews but also large factions of the German navy. Although it had been almost possible to replace vessels in sufficient numbers, it was not possible to replace experienced crews in quite the same way. Thus, the German High Command was forced to send out insufficiently trained crews, putting further vessels and men at unacceptable risk.

A ministry not often mentioned received prominence when Lord Beaverbrook directed the War Council to appoint Lord Northcliffe head of the Ministry of Information in February 1918. Not to be confused with any of the intelligence departments or censoring offices, its aims were the 'control of public opinion' and the 'influence of the vast Armies of Germany'. Its influence was on literature and radio transmissions in many languages throughout Europe. Operating from Crewe House, this Ministry was responsible for a vast propaganda campaign and network which distributed millions of leaflets behind enemy lines. Today, we are not inclined to give so much credence to the value of war propaganda, but there is no doubt that this Ministry played an extremely important role in the First World War. This view was endorsed at the end of the War by German General Lunderdorf who suggested that Lord Northcliffe was 'a master of mass suggestion' and contended that 'Germany was beaten not by arms, but by the moral collapse of the German soldiers produced by Lord Northcliffe's deadly propaganda'. This view was again reaffirmed later in the German Press: 'Unfortunately we cannot deny Lord

Northcliffe attained his aims, and he can leave the political arena in triumph'. As in the case of the Gulf War, the management of war reporting was and is seen to be essential.

Finally on 23 May 1918, after the failure of the German army's last major push on the Western Front, Prime Minister Lloyd George was able to announce: 'We are sinking U-boats faster than Germany can build them, and building ships faster than U-boats can sink them'. Given all of this, it was still no picnic for those afloat in the British and Irish Channels and attacks on and from both sides continued right up until Armistice Day.

The German Navy had been blocked and squeezed in all its theatres of operations. Although U-boat construction programmes were still flat out (on Armistice Day, there were 224 U-boats under construction in German yards), and many commanders still on 'aggressive patrol', it was obvious that with the completion of the mine barrage across the North Sea and the proposed intention to extend the principal to the Mediterranean, the game was up for the Germans. In October 1918, the U-boat bases at Flanders were evacuated and the once powerful and proud German Navy openly revolted, announcing its distaste for a continuation of the War. The Armistice was agreed shortly after on 11 November 1918.

Britain had gone to the brink of the 'precipice' in 1917, but with the aid of a powerful ally, she had soon pulled back - that is, until a very similar situation arose again during the next 'Great War'. After Germany surrendered in 1918, there was a veritable scramble by the Allies to seize what remained of the U-boat fleet in order to learn the secrets of these superior submarines. Despite this, when the Second World War commenced, the German U-boats again caught the Allies unprepared and dominated the Western Approaches.

Chapter 2
Queenstown - Kingstown: the connection

There had been widespread reporting of the 'cowardly attack' on the *Lusitania* off Queenstown and many saw this act as the reason for America entering the War. However, this was not the case and it was two more years before the USA committed itself to the War on the side of the Allies. In several ways, comparisons can be made between the sinking of the *Lusitania* and that of the *Leinster*. Although not an issue in the case of the *Lusitania*, both vessels were unescorted. Both vessels suffered massive secondary explosions attributed to the boilers. And of course, both attacks were perpetrated by the 'Murdering Hun'. Although many publications of investigations into early salvage work on the Lusitania revealed some clandestine cargoes such as munitions, gun mountings and so on, very little investigation has been carried out on the *Leinster*.

It was not until three years after the sinking of the Lusitania, in the very final days of the war, that the *Leinster* was torpedoed while en route from Kingstown to Holyhead, with disastrous consequences. Here again the Leinster was also said to be an innocent passenger ship playing no role in support of the war. Oddly enough, on the day following the sinking, Mr Balfour was almost too quick to make a very similar denial to that issued in the *Lusitania* affair: 'The *Leinster* was not carrying military stores'. Whether she was or not that day, she most certainly was on previous occasions. This is a fact supported by many corroborating entries in the *Leinster's* journals. Leaving aside cargoes, without doubt she was a legitimate target, if only because of the troops that were consistently conveyed on her to and from Britain. These were not troops in ones and twos but quite frequently hundreds. The fact that the authorities allowed such large numbers of troops to travel unescorted with civilians was in itself unforgiveable. But later attempts at disguising this fact from the public and trying to put the full responsibility for the attack on the 'Murdering Hun' in order to influence public opinion, was even more reprehensible.

Dotted right around the British Isles, there were numerous military and naval bases. Of these, Queenstown had become a principal player, being strategically situated on the Western Approaches. Whilst President of the Royal Naval College at Greenwich in 1915, Admiral Bayly was invited to take command of the Western Approaches. After some heated negotiations, he accepted the job provided that he was given full control of 'all the waters around Ireland and a fast destroyer'. These conditions were met and Admiral Bayly arrived at Queenstown in July 1915 aboard the light cruiser *HMS Adventure*. He received this flagship at a time when such vessels were becoming a valuable and very scarce resource.

Admiral Bayly was a master of destroyer tactics and although naval vessels other than converted ex-fishing boats were extremely scarce, he applied his skills vigorously with immediate results. He was a reserved and private person who fully appreciated the seriousness of the situation and despised idleness. Notwithstanding his apparent gruffness, he had a reputation for an ability to communicate firmly

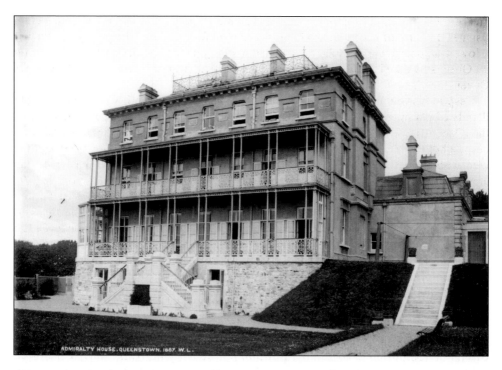

Admiralty House. The command centre at Queenstown where Admiral Bayly directed naval operations around Ireland during the First World War

The excellent facilities for the Fleet at Queenstown

and quietly, but equally important he w s found to be to be a warm and considerate listener. In spite of his reputation and his total enforcement of the policy 'no ladies' allowed on board war vessels, he retained a soft spot for his niece who assisted him at Queenstown. This was Miss Voycey who was warmly known as 'Queen Of Queenstown'.

Despite his preoccupation with Sinn Féin spies and their ability to relay valuable details of his operations to the enemy, he ultimately changed the poor reputation of the Queenstown Command. The base became of considerable import-ance, and despite his abhorrence of all publicity, he gained the respect of both his peers and the men who served under him. The status of the base was further enhanced with the arrival of the US Navy at Queenstown in 1917. American ser-vicemen also had the height of praise for Admiral Bayly and have long since commemorated the friendships and operations which both navies and countries shared during the war. (Not all American naval officers saw eye to eye with their Royal Navy counterparts.)

The USA finally threw in its lot with the Allies in April of 1917. A short time prior to the actual declaration of war with Germany, Admiral Sims travelled incognito from America to Britain with instructions from the American Chief of Naval Operations that confirmed an American reluctance to enter the war: 'Don't let the British pull the wool over your eyes. It is none of our business pulling their chestnuts out of the fire. We would as soon fight the British as the Germans'. Having been earlier taken in by British propaganda, when Admiral Sims arrived in Britain he soon discovered that the position was actually far worse than he had been led to believe. It was alarmingly clear that extremely urgent action was re-quired. Even at that late stage, he remarked that the population of Britain appeared to know nothing of the gravity of the situation and the true peril that the country was then in. He noted that hotels and theatres seemed to be packed each night with merrymakers.

Following several subsequent meetings between US navy commanders and the British Admiralty, an urgently required flotilla of six United States Navy (USN) destroyers was dispatched for Queenstown, Cork. As the number of U-boat attacks had been steadily rising, this news came as a great relief to the war-weary sailors of Queenstown, but as no real surprise, as sightings of armed US merchantmen had been regularly increasing.

The Queenstown base became pivotal in the control of the triangle bounded by south-west Ireland, Milford Haven and the Scilly Isles. From here, intelligence from all around Ireland was gathered and co-ordinated, and operational orders were dispatched, including instructions to the auxiliary base at Kingstown. On 4 May 1917, Admiral Bayly ordered *ML 181* to proceed west from Queenstown to rendez-vous with and escort the eagerly awaited USN destroyers to port.

Aboard *ML 181* were several high ranking officers, one of whom may be famil-iar to Irish subaqua divers. This was the young and recently promoted Captain Evans. Captain Evans was held in such high esteem that at the special request of Admiral Sims, he was appointed Chief Liaison Officer to the US Forces. This was a man of adventure who left his mark in every sphere of life in which he engaged. From being a Royal Navy volunteer on the great exploits with Scott's Polar explorations, to the praiseworthy notoriety received in the Dover Strait only one month previous. While stationed at Dover, he received the title of '*Evans Of The Broke*' as a result of a raid by six German destroyers in the Dover Strait where they encountered the two British ships *Broke* and *Swift*. The Broke sank one and rammed another destroyer, after which hand to hand combat continued on decks. Thereafter the engagement became known as *'The Broke'* incident.

When the First World War ended, Captain Evans continued his service in the navy and in 1921 received the first ever gold medal from Lloyds for a magnificent and heroic rescue in the China Seas. Captain Evans continued an illustrious career in service through both World Wars with more than just a smattering of charm and good fortune. Another of his adventures occurred some thirty years later when the Norwegian *MV Bolivar* was approaching Dublin on the last leg of her maiden voyage and once again Evans escaped serious misfortune. March 1947 has long been remembered for its severity, and it was during the freezing stormy night of 4 March that the 6,000 ton motor vessel Bolivar grounded on the Kish Bank and broke in two. Aboard was none other than Captain Evans (by then Lord Mountevans) accompanied by his charming wife and an entourage of about a dozen, who by later accounts, were none too upset by the snowstorm nor their predicament. It was rumoured in the newspapers at the time that it might have been more the fine food and boisterous celebrations aboard the ship the previous night, and less shifting sands of the Kish Bank that ensnared the *Bolivar*. However, the crew and passengers sat it out until the next day when they were rescued by vessels from both Dublin Port and Dun Laoghaire.

When the first flotilla of six US destroyers arrived at Queenstown, they were greeted warmly by the local inhabitants who cheered from the surrounding hilltops. No one was more relieved at the sight of the US Navy and the significance of their commitment than Admiral Bayly and he immediately put the destroyers under his command. As was his custom, he wasted no time putting them to sea and 'on patrol'. The USA was thus totally committed and Queenstown saw many more arrivals of American naval vessels. Although the US Navy maintained a certain parallel 'autonomy' under Admiral Sims, both British and American navies displayed a remarkable spirit of togetherness, operating as one under the Admiral.

The US forces also won considerable popularity with the local ladies and a little more with the commercial interests of Cork city, until a regrettable and serious incident occurred. Some say that it was local Sinn Féin members who were making life difficult for the American servicemen and some said it was just plain jealous menfolk with their noses out of joint. In any event, an incident developed between a local lass, a US serviceman and the girl's fiancé. The result was a scrap, after which the fiancé died. The case went to court, following which all visits by enlisted servicemen to Cork were terminated. Despite repeated submissions from the Lord Mayor of Cork, Admiral Bayly would not reverse the confinement. However, this did not prevent the girls travelling to Queenstown, especially at weekends. It was not long before the US Navy and the envy that its relatively well-paid ratings evoked reached the shores of Scotland. At places like Inverness and Invergordon, it is said that the young ladies ran wild with sailors of the 'Millionaire Navy'. So much so, that Admiral Sims took the very same action as Bayly and confined the sailors to their base! The situation pertaining to US servicemen abroad lead to tensions once more during the Second World War. The affect American garrisons had on local economies and local ladies is well known and is captured in the song Rum And Coca Cola which was attributed to such a situation in Trinidad:

> *When soldier go parading by*
> *Native girls all wink the eye*
> *Help soldier celebrate his leave*
> *Make every day like New Year's Eve ...*
> *Both mother and daughter singing for the Yankee dollar.*

The 'new' Command at Queenstown, with less than adequate resources, began a task that was daunting. Tactics and the most effective use of the available vessels were of paramount importance if the new Command was to stem the rapid advances of the German U-boats. There was an enormous expanse of ocean to patrol and the Command's tasks were to hunt and destroy or capture enemy submarines and shipping. In addition, it was necessary to both fine tune and provide escorts for the newly introduced convoy system. A convoy system had not been operated since the early nineteenth century and its reintroduction was not possible until the US threw in with the allies. But when initiated, the operation became an instant success. It marked a turning point in the war at which shipping losses began a significant decline and continued to do so until the war ended.

The convoy system was quite complicated in its operational details. Put simply, it meant that groups of similar vessels loaded with supplies, men and machinery gathered at predetermined assembly points. They were issued with detailed sailing instructions and then travelled in convoy to their destination under an escort of a screen of destroyers. At certain points during the convoy's journeys, the dangers of attack increased, such as the Western Approaches and the South and North coasts of Ireland. These were areas where the convoys bunched and slowed as they came close to the Channels and the major ports. In so doing, they created a convenient shooting gallery for German commanders. It was in these areas that losses had been heavy and where the US navy destroyers and fast patrol boats were urgently required. They operated in all weathers - fair and quite often extremely foul.

Their intervention had an immediate impact on the freedom U-boats had enjoyed in attacking merchant shipping. It became almost impossible for them to penetrate the screens of destroyers without great risk to themselves. This led to a change of tactics by the submarine commanders. The U-boats soon began to focus their attention on the areas where the convoys reached the 'danger zones' of the George's and North Channels. Also very popular with persistent submarine commanders was the Irish Sea. To reach this area it meant not only a difficult and dangerous entry through the well-patrolled entrances to the Irish Sea, but also an even more dangerous exit. Any delay after attack in the Irish Sea meant a strong possibility of being sighted and the risk of attacks from dreaded depth charges. It may have been possible to sneak by the patrols on entering the Irish Sea, but making an exit was even more tricky as the patrols knew that after an attack in the Channel, the submarine must pass their way.

The risks were high but so too were chances of success. Here in the middle of the Irish Sea, U-boats could lie in wait for slower cross channel traffic or merchant ships passing to the major industrial ports on the West coast of Britain after dispersing from their convoy, or for ships travelling from smaller ports to designated ones to assemble for convoy. At this point, merchant ships quite often sailed alone and thus became a more attractive target for a submarine attack. In order to defend themselves, many merchant ships were fitted with guns similar to the 12 pounder mounted on the Leinster's poop deck. This tactic, although defensive in its conception and application, actually proved to be offensive as far as U-boat commanders were concerned. It had the immediate affect of forcing the U-boats underwater and compelling their commanders who had until then enjoyed virtually risk free surface attacks on lone merchantmen, to make their attacks with valuable torpedoes. This resulted in lower kill ratios and reduced the sub's effectiveness more quickly. It also increased the frequency of U-boat cruises which in themselves were always dangerous. For the merchant ship, it rarely occasioned the use of its new armament.

The poor people of Ireland had hardly come to terms with the sight of people riding around in the new motor cars when they had to deal with canvas covered machines buzzing about in the skies. Assisting the patrol of the oceans was a new application of airships and a pioneering use of aeroplanes. These early military aircraft were a late arrival to Ireland, but a very welcome one for Admiral Bayly. There were a number and variety of bases established by the Royal Navy Airship Service around Ireland but the main ones were at Berehaven, Queenstown, Wexford and Lough Foyle. The role these aircraft played was confined mainly to escorting convoys and patrolling for submarines. Their significance had only begun to be appreciated when the War ended, but the experience of hunting from the air proved to be invaluable and extremely effective when it came to the next great conflict with German U-boats in the Second World War.

In the fight from the air, an interesting development in Ireland was the establishment by the United States Naval Air Service of several seaplane stations at a number of locations around the coast. Begun late in 1917 by the Royal Naval Air Service, this project was taken over by the United States Navy Air Service who completed the stations and supplied them with the Curtis 'Large America' flying boats. The buildings and materials were shipped to Queenstown and Dublin and transported by rail and road to the stations. The principal supply depot was at 76, Sir John Rogerson's Quay (still standing today) and was called the USN Aviation Supply Base. From here the USNAS was ideally situated, close to Dublin Port and all the railway connections on which supplies were rapidly deployed to the air stations throughout Ireland. The 'Large America' was just that, nearly 50 feet long with four machine guns and as many bombs. The USN stations in Ireland did not become viable until March 1918 and never really had a great effect on the War. Nevertheless, the establishment of structures, procedures and battle experience in this European outpost was invaluable to the US forces. At the close of the War, there were as many as 1,500 officers and servicemen of that branch of the US navy billeted at Queenstown alone.

Curtis Flying Boat being launched at Cork

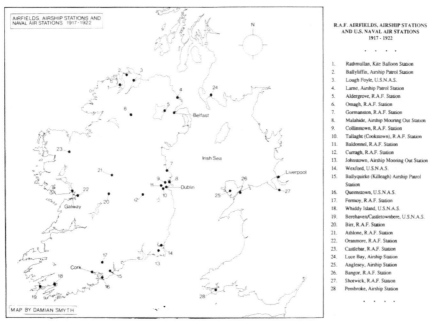

A map of the various air bases around Ireland in the First World War

A mine layer under escort from an airship out of Wexford

The overall command for the flying wing of the US Navy in Europe was known as the USN Aviation Forces, Foreign Service and was commanded by none other than Captain H.I. Cone who was headquartered at Paris and later at London. As the story unfolds, we will see the role this extremely popular career officer played in the *Leinster* tragedy while he was inspecting these air bases in Ireland.

Although hard pressed, there were a variety of methods and craft at the disposal of Admiral Bayly with which to patrol the seas around the British Isles. Airships, aeroplanes, Trap or 'Q' ships, submarines, converted merchantmen and ex-fishing vessels and of course the desperately needed destroyers. These waters were divided into 'sectors' or 'squares'. During the earlier years of the War, the size of an area a destroyer had to patrol was sometimes as large as 1,500 square miles. From 1917, with the provision of additional craft, this figure was dramatically reduced. Within any area, a 'patrol' was responsible for the safe passage of shipping and the hunting of enemy submarines. This method of division and allocation of sea areas had both advantages and disadvantages. An advantage was that a skipper or shore listener could easily focus on a relevant sector if just the special code for that area was transmitted. Even though the instant satellite navigation system that is available today was not in use then, it was possible to provide positioning to vessels by way of 'radio fixes'. For example, if a vessel was attacked, it had only to transmit its approximated sector or square code and shore based listeners could then home in on the signal to provide a position to the skipper and the nearest patrol. However, a disadvantage earlier in the War was that observant U-boat skippers could anticipate where a patrol craft might be at any given time before variation was introduced into patrol patterns. This system of areas, sectors and squares operated up into the Irish sea and included the cross channel mail route. The early chart shown and taken from *Beating The U-boats* by E. K. Chatterton may have been updated sometime later than April 1917 as the areas seem to differ from ones that have been researched and does not include the mail boat route which was SQ-72.

Here in this narrow and often angry Irish Sea existed a most important link. It was the Kingstown-Holyhead mail boat route and was operated by four advanced steamers owned by The City of Dublin Steam Packet Co. Contemporary and updated hydrographic charts covering the Irish Sea did not seem to be available to the Germans, but this same area was known to them as 'Quadrant 524 J'. Instinctively, and with only the one exception in the case of the South Arklow Light Vessel, none of the navigation lights were interfered with by U-boats. Although the Irish Sea narrows to about twenty miles outside Belfast, here it is sixty miles wide consisting of open and deep water into which German submarines had been marauding with near impunity.

Supplementing this link was another very interesting network of transportation. This was the deep water and fleet facilities at Queenstown which were directly connected by rail to the Port of Dublin and the mail steamers at Carlisle Pier, Kingstown. Kingstown harbour also had sidings to the Traders and Victoria Wharves where there were extensive facilities for the Admiralty which included a naval munitions depot. The main line was owned and operated by the Great Southern and Western Railway Co. which had facilitated the transport of trans-Atlantic mails from and to Britain and Ireland. A strategic concept of an earlier

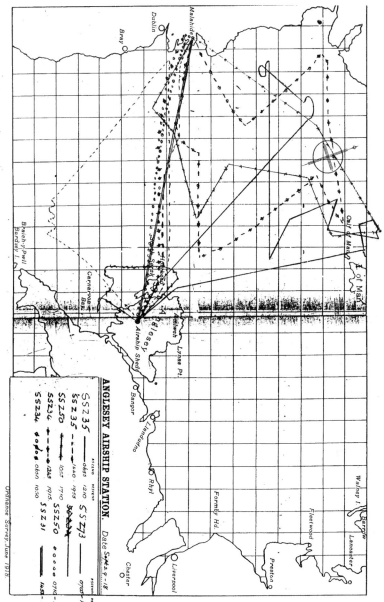

Airship patrol patterns over the Irish Sea on 29 September 1918. This was the day following the sinking of the SS Baldersby near the Codling Light Vessel

time, it passed through a number of counties with important military installations, like that of the considerable training camp at The Curragh, Co. Kildare. Military journeys to and from these camps had normally been facilitated from the 'military platform' at Kingsbridge station, but could extend beneath the Phoenix Park, connecting to the Port of Dublin and the harbour at Kingstown. Ultimately there

THE CITY OF DUBLIN STEAM
PACKET CO.'S
ROYAL MAIL SERVICE
Between IRELAND & ENGLAND
(Via KINGSTOWN and HOLYHEAD).
SEA PASSAGE, 2 HOURS, 45 MINUTES.

Through communication between Cork and all
Principal English Stations, leaving Cork 3.30 p.m.
Through Tickets via Mail, can be obtained at 15
Eden Quay, as well as at the Railway Booking Offices.

DUBLIN (North Wall) TO
LIVERPOOL.
SEA PASSAGE 8 HOURS.
THROUGH BOOKING
For Passengers, Goods, etc.
EVERY WEEK-DAY, 8 p.m.

Fares:—Saloon, . Return (available 6
Single .... 13/6 · months .... 21/·
Deck .... 5/· Do. Do. Do. ... 8/·

On EVERY FRIDAY and SATURDAY CABIN EXCUR-
SION TICKETS are issued for the Double Journey,
available for return any week-day within sixteen days
from date of issue. Saloon, 16s; Deck, 7s 6d.
A Daily Omnibus Service is run in connection with
the Company's Steamers and English Railways.

A52971

Newspaper advertisement of the Royal Mail Service

was a complete network and access to or from any of the major towns in the United Kingdom and across the Irish Sea to any of those in Ireland.

A curious fact throughout the War was, that although this network of travel and distribution was a key factor in the distribution of men and materials, the security of this network in Ireland (with the exception of the threat by U-boats on traffic across the Irish Sea) never seems to have been under any serious threat.

The harbour facilities at Kingstown were quite a valuable asset, not only to the City of Dublin and Steam Packet Co. but also strategically important to the Admiralty at the outbreak of the war. Until then the Admiralty had enjoyed some lesser onshore facilities and moorings for the Reserve Fleet in the more protected bight of the East Pier. Kingstown had several advantages of size, direct and unimpeded access to the Irish Sea and was considered to be the only harbour outside Queenstown to have its entrance protected by an armed fort. Dublin Port may seem to have been a logical choice but it necessitated long journeys at reduced speed in and out of the river. In addition, the memory of disloyal labour unrest in the General Strike of 1913 had not yet been put to bed.

It was not until 1915 that the Admiralty began to extend its facilities at Kingstown, providing additional accommodation and munitions storage capacity in the area of Victoria Wharf. In the areas of the Coal Quay and Traders Wharf, dredging was proposed for additional berthage and mooring for patrol boats. Eventually the whole of the Victoria Wharf area was sealed off in favour of the Admiralty and a first rate auxiliary naval base was established. The communications network was also well situated with the main South East telephone trunk accessible on the nearby railway line, alongside a cross channel telegraph link which came ashore at Kilcoole. There was also a telegraph office at Kingstown and telephone connections direct to Dublin also via the railway routes. The naval station had access to naval wireless, telephone, shipping, road and rail facilities and was situated in the heart of a town filled with a loyalist and patriotic fervour.

By October 1918 there was one light cruiser, eleven British and seven US destroyers and submarine chasers operating from here and Holyhead. They operated under the title of the Irish Sea Hunting Flotilla and covered an area of 180 miles North to South. In addition, there were a very large number of lesser vessels and patrol craft all under the command of Flag Captain Campbell VC at Holyhead. Serving under Captain Campbell was Commodore John Denison who was in charge of the auxiliary base at Kingstown.

So well situated was Kingstown as a naval base that when the War ended, it was proposed to shift the naval headquarters at Queenstown to Kingstown. It became extremely difficult for the authorities to dislodge the Admiralty from this enclave which had become known as the 'Gateway To Ireland'. The importance of such a base was further enhanced during the Irish Rebellion of April 1916. After insurrection had broken out around the country, the Port of Dublin was sealed and the gun boat HMS Helga was ordered to patrol up the Liffey. On 25 April the mail boat Ulster was signalled at Holyhead and ordered to divert to Liverpool. Shortly after the Ulster cleared Holyhead, she proceeded north, and the following was recorded by Captain Newton in the ship's journal: 'Sailed light for troops'. After turning about in Liverpool the same day, she sailed not for the heart of the troubled city of Dublin, but for Kingstown with '1277 troops as per log'. After disembarkation at Kingstown, she turned about after coaling and again sailed for Liverpool on 26 April 'light for troops'. At Liverpool '834 troops boarded', accompanied this time by a large quantity of munitions. The entry in the journal records the cargo in this way: 'Ammunition and 834 grenades. A large quantity of small ammunition. A large quantity of 18 pound shells for quick firing. About 90 tons in all'. The Ulster sailed and made Kingstown again on 26 April. On 27 April, it returned to Liverpool a third time, again 'light for troops'. At Liverpool '869 troops' embarked and returned to Kingstown the same day. On 28 April, the *Ulster* sailed for Liverpool but received instructions en route and diverted to Holyhead where it later returned to normal service on 5 May.

Throughout this period, the Leinster was out of service and normal packet service was operated by the only remaining Province, the Munster. The question would seem to arise of why the troops were not transported directly to the troubles in the centre of Dublin? It may simply be that for the operation of landing troops and munitions, it was necessary to have a secure landing area - and where better than Kingstown? Soon afterwards the naval authorities at Kingstown congratulated the harbour and OPW staff for their help in the 'late trouble'. Obviously not all of the citizens of Ireland were in support of the Rebellion. The valuable connections at Kingstown had not always been accessible to the City of Dublin Steam Packet Company (CDSP Co.). Up until 1859, the mails and passengers could only be transported the six miles from the Victoria Wharf and Carlisle Pier at Kingstown on the privately run Kingstown and Dublin Railway as far as Westland Row. Things improved in 1891 after several railroad and interested companies, including CDSP Co. contributed to the construction of the Tara Street Loop Line Bridge across the Liffey. This gave the company nearly total access to the extensive all-Ireland railway system. To complete access, it needed to connect with the existing

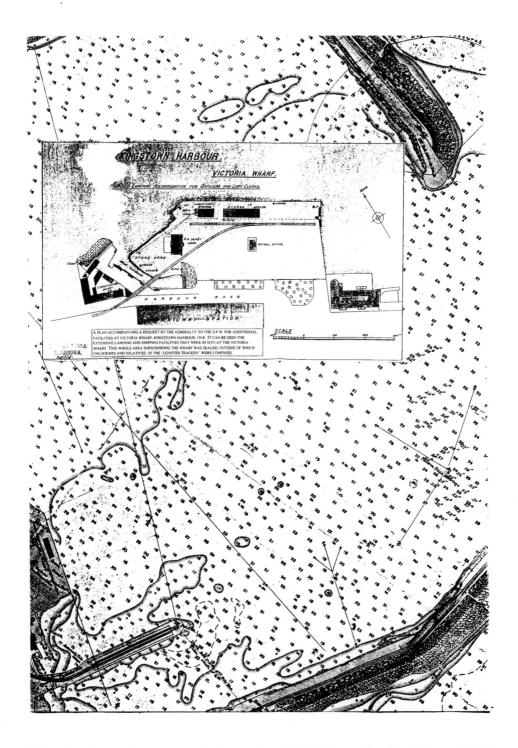

Admiralty chart of Kingstown harbour dated 1902. In use by the Office of Public Works and the naval base at Kingstown

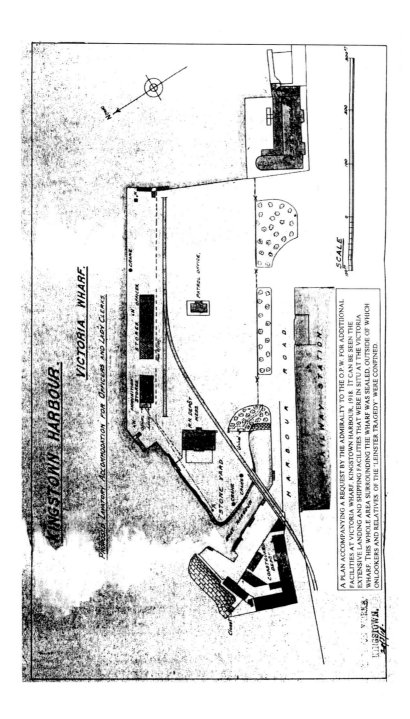

A plan accompanying a request by the Admiralty to the OPW for additional facilities at Victoria Wharf, Kingstown, 1918. The whole area surrounding the Victoria Wharf was sealed off, outside of which onlookers and relatives of those who suffered in the Leinster tragedy were confined

PUBLIC WORKS
IRELAND
3272
12 MAY 1916

H.M. NAVAL BASE, KINGSTOWN.

11th May 1916.

No.74.   Sir,

I wish to convey to the Board my appreciation
of the way the men belonging to the Irish Board of Works,
under their foreman, Mr Travers, assisted at the dis-
-embarkation of the troops at the Victoria Quay, Kingstown,
during the late trouble, and also my thanks for all the
assistance received from their Officials.

The Chairman.
Mr. Commr. Hanson.
Mr. Commr. LeFanu.

I am,

Sir,

Your obedient Servant,

CAPTAIN IN CHARGE.

THE SECRETARY,

OFFICE OF PUBLIC WORKS.

DUBLIN.

ISSUED

Memorandum to the Secretary,
H.M. Naval Base,
Kingstown.

In reply to your enquiry I am to state that the following are
the approximate dates on which the various buildings were erected
on the Victoria Wharf, Kingstown Harbour, for the use of the
Admiralty:-

1.   Conversion of the Baggage Shed to a Store- April 1915

11.   Erection of offices at the eastern end of the Store
        January 1918

111.   Erection of an Ammunition Store March 1918

1V.   Fitting up Offices in Store 1 above, April 1918

V.   Erection of Lavatories at the western end of Store 1
        above, May 1918.

Secretary.

OFFICE OF PUBLIC WORKS,
DUBLIN, 12th NOVEMBER 1918.

Two letters of thanks from the Commander at Kingstown for help from workers at Kingstown during the 'late troubles'

28

line just north of Amiens Street station at a place which later became known as the 'Battle of Newcome Bridge' - the reference to a 'battle' rep-resents the continuing difficulties it was having with the Railway companies. Having gone to arbitration in 1892, the result went in favour of the company who then completed and consolidated its access to all of Ireland from all of England via the company's mail boats.

To a lesser extent the connection from Queenstown - Rosslare - Pembroke, or Dublin - Rosslare - Pembroke, was also used to convey troops and material but it never had the same prestige and degree of safety as that on the Kingstown - Holyhead route. This is in part due to the larger and easier operating area for enemy submarines in the George's and Bristol Channels, but mainly because of CDSPCo's fast and elusive steamers.

The importance is obvious of such a connection between Queenstown and Kingstown with all of their facilities, and the UK via the 'ferries'. The connection also had the distinct advantage of being less risky than journeying by way of the George's Channel or the South Irish Sea and was the quickest and preferred route by all manner of high ranking officers and gentlemen.

Chapter 3
The oldest steamship company in the world

*A plaque on the Old Seaman's
Mission 12-14 Eden Quay*

*The plaque on what were once the
offices of the CDSPCo.*

It is difficult to be absolutely certain when a regular mail packet service across the Irish Sea began. However, Ball's History of County Dublin records that at the beginning of the seventeenth century, a service did exist from Howth to Holyhead operated by Captain Pepper who 'passed to and fro like a light horseman'. This history also states that when the winds were unfavourable, Howth fishermen stepped in and carried 'letters to England in open row boats'. Conveyancing of the mail continued by sail until such a time as progress gave way to the revolutionary invention of steam powered vessels.

The vision of an Irish owned steamship company was born in 1815. This was the year when one of the earliest steamers, the Argyle, visited Dublin and sailed on to London with passengers and cargo. The implications were obvious. Shortly after, a group of Dublin businessmen were quick to recognise where the future of cross channel travel lay and formed the Steam Packet Company. Amongst this prominent group were Richard and Charles Wye Williams of Drumcondra Castle, sons of the Secretary of the Bank of Ireland. Born in 1779, the younger Charles, although qualified at the Bar, became absorbed by the potential applications of the new power of steam which had begun in ships and later co-founded the City of Dublin Steam Packet Company (CDSPCo.).

The Steam Packet Company later became the Dublin Steam Packet Company and its first vessel, the Hibernia, sailed from Dublin in 1816. A rash of steam shipping companies followed and somehow the Dublin Steam Packet Company faded into obscurity. However, the younger Charles, with a brilliance for things mechanical, began his own steamship company calling it after himself. This he later changed to The City of Dublin Steam Packet Company and sailed his first steamer across the Irish Sea in 1823. The vessel was sentimentally named the City of Dublin and was built by the Corkman, Thomas Wilson of Liverpool. The company operated its services from the quays at the Custom House only a short distance from its offices at 15, Eden Quay. Thankfully the company's crest is still preserved and prominent on the building's facade to this day.

The presumptuous entrance by Dublin businessmen into the new steamship business caused much upset to those still in sailing ships, not least of these being the London Post Office. The new technology the steamships brought to the business was, of course, just progress but the rancour it created with its competitors haunted the company, until it was finally consumed by it a century later.

In the interim CDSPCo. went from strength to strength, obtaining old companies and new routes throughout Europe. Its directors were far seeing and progressive and did not confine themselves entirely to the oceans. In 1828 the CDSPCo. absorbed the Inland Steam Navigation Company which had been established earlier by Charles Williams at Killaloe and extended the range and movement of goods, livestock and passengers throughout the Shannon and canal systems.

THE CITY OF DUBLIN STEAM PACKET COMPANY
FORWARD GOODS

By their Boats and Steam Vessels on the Grand Canal and River Shannon,

FROM DUBLIN TO		TO RETURN ON
Athlone on Tuesday and Friday,	at 5A.M.	Tuesday and Friday
Ballinasloe Tuesday, Thursday, Saturday,	5P.M.	Monday, Wednesday,, Friday,
Dromineer (Nenagh) Monday & Thursday,	5A.M.	Tuesday and Saturday,
Portumna Monday and Thursday	5A.M.	Tuesday and Saturday,
Killaloe Monday, Wednesday, Friday,	4P.M.	Tuesday, Thursday, Saturday
Limerick Monday, Wednesday, Friday	4P.M.	Monday, Wednesday, Friday,
Shannon Harbour Monday, Tuesday,		⎰ Tuesday, Wednesday, Fri-
Thursday, Friday,	5A.M.	⎱ day, Saturday,
Tullamore Monday, Tuesday, Thursday,		⎰ Monday, Wednesday,
Friday,	5A.M.	⎱ Thursday, Saturday.

Well-appointed Cattle Boats leave Portumna, Ballinasloe, and Shannon Harbour, every Week, with stock for the Dublin Market.

STORES,—CANAL HARBOUR, JAMES' STREET.
(OPPOSITE MARKET-STREET.)

at which place Shippers are requested to have their goods delivered before Three o'clock, to prevent delay in forwarding.

☞ The Boats of the Company travel by Night on the Grand Canal, and with the utmost despatch and regularity.

RATES OF FREIGHT may be ascertained on application at the Company's Offices, James'-street Harbour, and at 15 Eden-quay Dublin, or at the several stations of the Company.

A sample of early services offered by the CDSPCo.

During the years that followed, the company acquired and had built a huge fleet of vessels. In this, Mr Williams designed and contributed a number of engineering innovations which were adopted into the ships' design. One of the company's early vessels, the Royal William, was the first steamer to cross the North Atlantic from the Mersey without touching Ireland in 1838 and was also one of the earliest vessels to be fitted with iron watertight bulkheads. Charles Wye Williams and the CDSPCo. not only established steam vessels on inland waterways and on cross channel and trans-Atlantic routes, but were also in part responsible for the establishment of the great engineering company of Cammel Laird (then Laird's Birkenhead Iron Works) as shipbuilders. It was upon the establishment of the Inland Steam Navigation Co. at Killaloe (previously the Shannon Steam Packet Co.), that Charles Williams ordered a sixty foot iron barge to be built by William

31

Laird in 1829. Two more followed soon after. These were the first iron boats to be built on the Mersey.

In 1833, another first was completed by Laird's on the Mersey. This was the first all iron paddle steamer and was laid down in yard No. 1 for the CDSPCo. She was the 130 foot long *Lady Lansdowne* and was delivered in sections by a sailing ship to the Shannon. She was assembled at Killaloe where it remains beneath the water to this day. *The Lady Lansdowne* was followed in 1834 by the *Garryowen* which was probably the first vessel ever fitted with watertight bulkheads, a feature conceived and designed by Charles Wye Williams. This close and progressive relationship between the CDSPCo. and Cammel Lairds could only remain while both survived. Sadly, the CDSPCo. was first to go but was followed by the great shipbuilders a half century later.

The CDSPCo. also had its share of setbacks. In 1829, it lost two vessels, the *Manchester* and the *Britannia*. In 1841, the *Thames* was also lost and with it a serious toll of passengers. At the entrance to Dublin Port, the company lost its paddle steamer, the *Queen Victoria*, in 1853. Beneath the Bailey lighthouse, this 'Dreadful Shipwreck At Howth' claimed more than eighty lives. Under ordinary circumstances, the loss of such vessels was of no serious concern as they were well insured and easily replaced, but many years later, under circumstances that were extraordinary, the company suffered the loss of two vessels which forced it to cease trading.

An agent with the Inland Steam Navigation Company, William Wilson, became managing director of the parent CDSPCo. in 1849. This was one year prior to the company obtaining its first contract for the transportation of the Royal Mail across the Irish Sea. The Admiralty who had previously operated this contract ceased to do so and sold two of its mail vessels, the St Columba and the Llwywllyn to the CDSPCo. who continued to operate them on its newly won mail contract between Kingstown and Holyhead. This lucrative contract was won fair and square, but a bitter aftertaste was left in the boardroom at London and North Western Railways (LNWR), whose directors had behaved badly in the whole tendering procedure. It was ominous and heralded a sign of bitter competition which clouded every aspect of this cross channel business.

Although the vessels that were acquired from the Admiralty were paddle driven, they achieved 14-16 knots and the fastest crossing time then of four hours and sixteen minutes. Following cries for shorter cross channel times, applications were again invited in 1859 for the transportation of the mails and another round of acrimonious tendering began. Not content with just the rail transport part of the contract, the LNWR sought to gain the whole 'straight through' contract from London to Dublin. This would have brought complete control over the very valuable connection from London to Queenstown. LNWR failed and the conveyancing of the mails between Kingstown and Holyhead was again awarded to the CDSPCo. which was able to perform the sea crossing in three hours and forty-five minutes for an annual sum of £85,900 with a penalty of £1.14d for every minute's delay.

In order to continue successful operations with the possibility of further improvements in contract times, the CDSPCo. placed orders with shipyards for four new paddle steamers to be named after the Provinces of Ireland - *Ulster, Munster,*

Leinster and Connaught. Three of these were ordered from Laird Bros. of Birkenhead and the fourth order was placed with Samuda of Ravenhill. In keeping with the exemplary tradition of the company, these vessels were operated at the highest standards and gave excellent service. They even at times reduced the crossing to three hours and operated at an average speed of 16.5 knots.

Still not happy with just their rail portion of the mail contract, the LNWR, in 1883, renewed pressure on the Post Office for a faster 'straight through' service. The boardroom boys were seriously at work this time and the LNWR managed not only to win the contract, but also to have it transferred to its own existing berths in Dublin Port. This, in effect, meant a generous payment for little additional outlay or inconvenience as their ships were already plying this route. Controversy exploded and a public outcry followed after which the decision was reversed in favour of the CDSPCo. During these protestations, William Watson died and was replaced on the board by his son of the same name.

After a time, pressure for a further decrease in the mail delivery times arose once more, and despite a complicated tendering procedure, the CDSPCo. again prevented the LNWR from obtaining the whole contract for a new 'Accelerated Service' in 1895. This was an extraordinary period between the two rival companies and somehow came to represent in microcosm the antipathy that existed between Ireland and England. The LNWR was seen to represent all that was British while on the other hand, the CDSPCo. was seen to represent Ireland's attempt to achieve a commercially viable and independent entity. The cartoon from the publication Lepracaun represents the difficulty the CDSPCo. had in obtaining berthage at the North Wall. It depicts John Bull, or the LNWR, as the bulldog in the manger keeping at bay the CDSPCo. or the victimised Irish, in the ripe milch cow.

The operations of the cross channel business were closely scrutinised. Practically every day there appeared in the daily papers some remark or other on the efficiency of the steamers and delivery times of the mails - almost to the point of obsession. The CDSPCo. had many enemies 'at court' and these needed only time to direct the contract elsewhere. There was so much public comment on the operations and conveyancing of the mails during the period of the contracts that the company kept ten hefty volumes of news clippings related to the subject. Despite persistent sniping from their main rival the LNWR, the CDSPCo. prevailed and received the contract for the next twenty years at an annual fee of £100,000. It was clear that this contract would see them well into the following century and, accordingly, a new generation of vessels was required.

The *Provinces*

Once more an order went to the shipyards of Laird Bros., this time for four identical twin screw steamers, pioneering the very latest design techniques. In keeping with Laird's traditional policy of high standards, the keels of this new generation of vessels were laid down in yard numbers 611, 612, 613 and 614 and meticulously overseen until their completion. After William Watson (Jnr, knighted

SPECIFICATION

OF

TWIN SCREW MAIL AND PASSENGER STEAMER

FOR THE

City of Dublin Steam Packet Company.

Dimensions.

Length over all - - - - -	372'	0"
Length on water line - - -	351'	6"
Breadth moulded - - - -	41'	6"
Depth at side—Upper deck - -	29'	3"
Main deck - - -	21'	4¾"
Deck house roof - -	36'	6"
Length of deck houses together - - about	178'	0"
Height of upper 'tween decks, beam to beam at middle	8'	8"
at side	7'	10½"
Tonnage B.M. - - - -	3,069 Tons	

Draft of water with 100 tons deadweight of Passengers and Mails, with coal in bunkers sufficient for a double trip (from bottom of bar keel) not to exceed - - - - - -   14' 6"

Engines.

Two independent sets of direct acting Triple Expansion Screw Engines with boilers to work under forced draught.

Trial Speed.

Speed on trial over an agreed base in fine weather during three hours run with not exceeding 90 tons of dead weight over and above the ship's tackle and furniture, - - - -   23 knots.

The Vessel to be fully equal to the present Mail Packets in steadiness, stability, and seaworthiness. All parts of the interior of the Hull to be reasonably accessible for scaling and painting. All lining to be put up with screws so that it can be easily taken down for this purpose. The machinery to be so arranged that all parts may be easily accessible and easy of repair and replacement, all the parts of the Engines of one Vessel being interchangeable with the Engines of the other Vessels.

Page 1 of the building contract for the Leinster *indicating special emphasis on the interchangeable machinery*

23

Signals

One set of cotton powder distress signals, 12 in number in box, with friction tubes and gun metal socket to be provided.
12 Blue lights.
2 Holme's deck flares.
6 Life buoy lights.

Hose

10 30-Feet lengths 2¼ inch copper riveted leather delivery hose, with the Company's regulation couplings lashed in.
1 Swan neck.
2 Directing pipes.
2 Hose keys.

Binnacles and Compasses

3 Brass binnacles and compasses, with brass dome top and lamps complete—one of "Moore's" or other approved make, and the others to be liquid compasses. One to be placed on house forming second-class entrance.
1 Spare suspended compass in box.
1 Pair glasses.

SHIP CHANDLERY STORES.

2 Deep-sea Leads, 30 lbs. each.	6 Scrapers.
1 do. Line.	4 Marline Spikes.
1 do. Reel.	12 Holystones and 6 handles.
2 Hand Leads.	6 Deck Scrubs.
2 do. Lines, 25 fathoms.	6 Paint Brushes.
2 Log Lines, 120 fathoms each.	6 do. Scrubs.
2 do. Ships.	6 Tar Brushes.
1 do. Reel.	4 Paint Cans.
2 do. Glasses.	1 Brass Speaking-trumpet.
12 Life-buoys.	1 Holme's Fog Horn "Aurora"
8 Cork Fenders.	12 Teak Buckets for fire purposes,
6 Mats.	with brass hoops, in suitable racks.
6 Mops.	12 Oak Deck Buckets.
6 Swabs.	1 do. Water Funnel.

Cooking Range and Utensils

A suitable iron cooking range with two fires and two ovens and funnel complete, of approved plan.

Page 23 of the same building contract indicating the attention paid to the smallest of ship's equipment

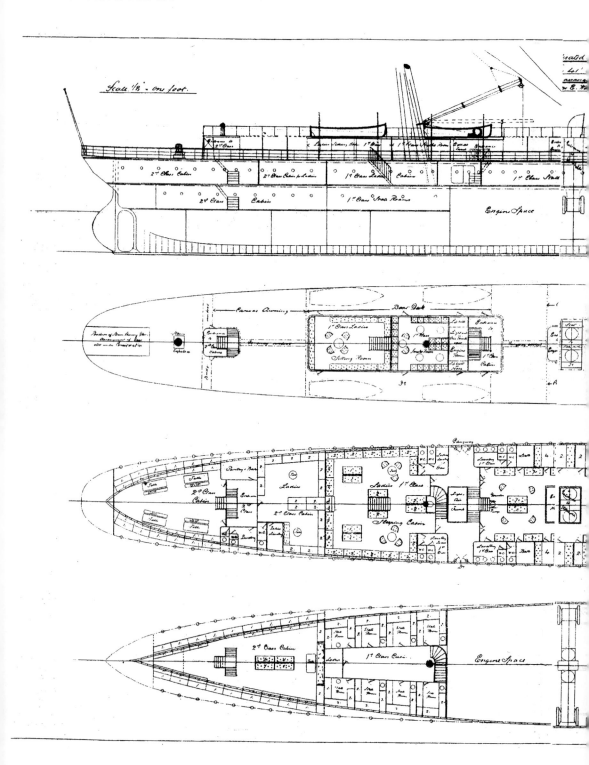

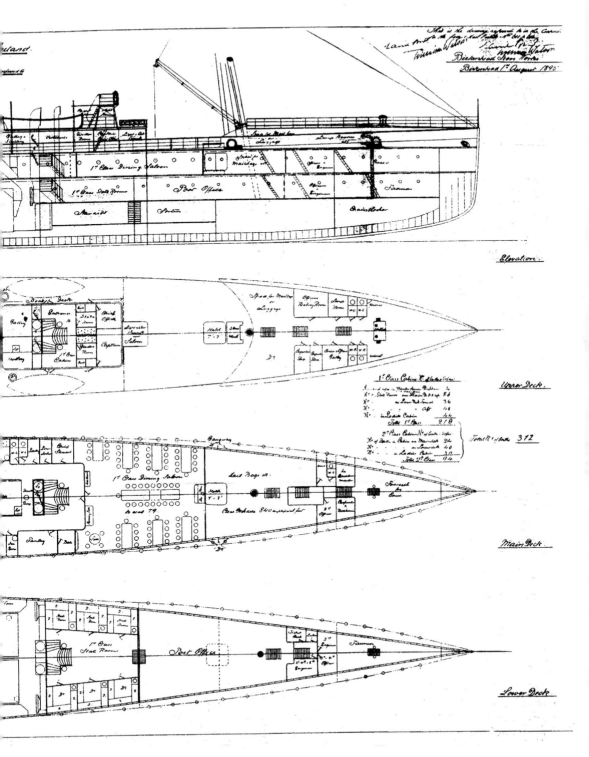

The decks' layout for the mailboat Leinster

What are believed to be photographs of the interior of one of the Provinces

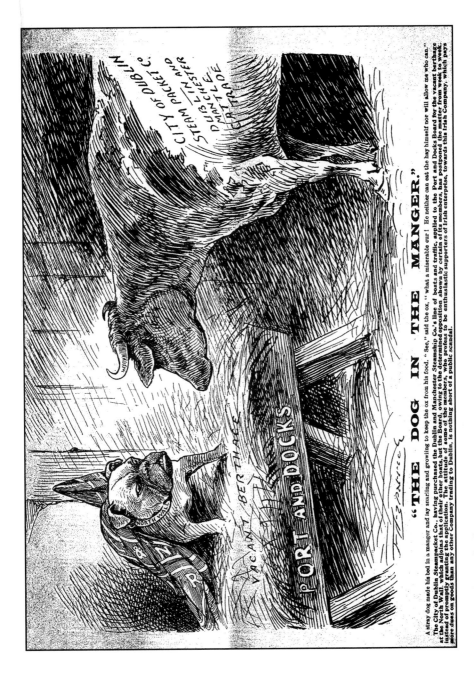

A sketch from the Lepracaun

in 1897) signed the agreement with Laird's in 1895, these four steamers became the most advanced of their kind. They quickly gained the reputation of not only being the fastest vessels on the Irish Sea but also the fastest channel steamers in the world and won for the City of Dublin Steam Packet Co. the envy and respect of the maritime industry.

Each ship grossed 2,641 tons and had three decks contained in an overall length of 372 feet with a moulded breadth of 42 feet. The dimensions indicate a 'narrow' ship, which indeed they were, and as a result they were later quite often mistaken for destroyers. The new design included twelve watertight compartments, two of which were through to the upper deck, and seven to the main deck with the makers claiming that 'even if two of these filled with water, the ship would still float' (not the first or the last useless boast of this nature). Speed being a critical factor of their operation, the hull was constructed of mild 'pickled' steel and the ships exceeded their specified speed of 23 knots by one knot. A notable feature of their construction was the 'turtle back' or 'hurricane' fo'c'sle which extended seventy feet aft, almost to the bridge. This feature of the ships' design, which can be seen today in ocean going fishing vessels, was particularly useful when ploughing through heavy seas at high speeds. Such rough journeys were often made to deliver the mails on time or to avoid submarines lying in wait. These ships made remarkable achievements, losing practically no time to rough weather (except for fog) or machinery breakdown.

The four ships were initially licensed to carry 1,400 passengers but never carried this many until the outbreak of the war. Passengers aboard any of the *Four Provinces* could travel in two classes and in superior conditions to any other cross channel ferry. Accommodation was contained in three decks - lower, middle and upper - with the 'boat deck' over the upper deck. Within the upper deck were three large 'deck houses'. These contained the first class entrance hall and a spacious smoke room decorated with oak in a Jacobean style. This was furnished with 'cosy seats equipped with arm and head rests'. Aft was the very comfortable ladies saloon or 'sitting room', decorated with white and gold in a Louis XVI style. Below, in the main deck, there were several cabin sections, state rooms and for-ward there was a splendid dining room or main saloon measuring 40 feet by 34 feet in which eighty people could enjoy fine food around a coal fire. Access to this area was through a handsome vestibule and stairway. All of this was decorated with mahogany in a Sheraton style. If you needed to retire, there were sleeping cabins mainly on the middle and lower decks with sixteen state rooms throughout.

The agreed 1895 layout of the ships' design show the galley and scullery on the upper deck aft of the bridge area with a lift to the main saloon. Forward in the bridge area were the officers' quarters and state rooms for the companies' directors. Although not shown on the original drawings, it is here that the radio officers quarters must have been located. (Photographs of the Provinces do not reveal any wireless aerials until the outbreak of the war.) Over this area on the boat deck was the chart room and wheelhouse. Further forward in the lower and middle decks was situated the generous mail sorting facilities. This area could accom-modate thirty postal workers and up to 250 bags of mail. The ship's furniture and fittings were of an exceptionally robust and high standard. During construction, detailed collaboration took place between the CDSPCo. and Laird's which resulted

THE LAUNCH OF THE LEINSTER, THE NEW IRISH MAIL STEAMER: THE COUNTESS OF CADOGAN NAMING THE VESSEL.

The launch of the Leinster *from* The Daily Graphic *14 September 1896*

in innovative design features, not least of which included particular attention to ventilation of accommodation and well concealed machinery.

Like their predecessors, these four vessels were again named *Ulster, Munster, Leinster and Connaught*. The only difference between the two sets was that the later ships' names were preceded with TSS. Unabbreviated this would read Twin Screw Steamer. This was their technical title, but they also appeared with their company abbreviation RMS, which is short for Royal Mail Steamer.

The first of the vessels to be launched from yard No. 611 was the *Ulster*. Accompanied by great ceremony and celebrations, the Duke and Duchess of Abercorn christened the Ulster at Laird's in June 1896. On this occasion, the Duchess Lady Hamilton had no inclination as to the terrible and ironic tragedy that would befall a close family relative. The Duchess was accompanied by her ten year old daughter Phyllis. In the adjacent yard, number 613, some three months later, the Countess of Cadogan named and launched the *Leinster*. It was not until twenty-two years later that a twist of fate sank that very same ship, with the grown but still young Lady Phyllis Hamilton and her two servants. All three lost their lives in the *Leinster* tragedy. The Munster was launched on 21 October 1896 and was followed by the Connaught in 1897.

Each of the four vessels was launched at Birkenhead at a cost of £95,905 amid great celebration and publicity. Notable dignitaries included Dublin's Lord Mayor and Mayoress, who congratulated the builders on the most modern innovations in machinery and comfort. The *Leinster's* maiden voyage had on board William Mason, the chairman of the CDSPCo., when she broke the existing record time of 2 hours and 30 minutes between Kingstown and Holyhead by six minutes. This

There were many depictions of the Provinces. Above is the first paddle-driven Leinster *and below is the 1895 'accelerated' version*

was measured lighthouse to lighthouse and was truly remarkable, when you consider that this record was only substantially improved upon by the best time of 1 hour and 30 minutes by the super high speed *HSS Stena Explorer* one hundred years and many billions of pounds later! As already mentioned, the *Provinces* had proved to be an excellent investment with very little, if any, time lost while delivering the mails. This was in the main due to the very efficient manner with which their captains ran the vessels. It was indeed a tribute to the company and its staff that in the all of the years in which these vessels operated, they lost only one knot on their average speed, i.e., from 19 to 18 knots.

The company prospered almost without event until 1908 when its old rival LNWR moved vessels from the Liffey to Kingstown in direct competition with the company. All manner of feathers were ruffled and the inevitable tussles for berthage broke out at the Carlisle Pier. The CDSPCo. received support at this time from the unusual quarter of Sinn Féin who quite rightly pointed out that the interference was a threat to Irish jobs. This unharmonious situation continued until the Admiralty requisitioned the LNWR vessels at the outbreak of the war in 1914. For the time being anyway, exempt from such seizures under the protection of their mail contract, it appeared at last that the CDSPCo would have some peace. It was not so, for the LNWR later moved vessels from Greenore to the Liffey just to keep their opponents honest. This was also the period of the great James Larkin and the labour troubles of 1913-14. It was as a result of the protracted dockers' labour dispute that the CDSPCo. lost a man who later might have become one of its most important allies.

Representing the employers was the tenacious and powerful William Murphy, a man with many commercial interests, one of which was ownership of Independent Newspapers. He effectively beat the strike and James Larkin, forcing dockers to return to work unconditionally. This was in contrast with a deal that James Larkin had negotiated with the CDSPCo. only some months earlier. At that time he took on the CDSPCo. for better wages and conditions and won. He subsequently broke this agreement when he became embroiled in the bitter 'lockout' with William Murphy. All was lost when the *Freeman's* journalist at the North Wall reported on 17 January that workers from the CDSPCo., 'the oldest steamship company in the world', were returning to work and agreeing to handle all cargoes alongside 'free labour'. It is conceivable that if James Larkin had not involved the CDSPCo. and won his battle with the establishment, he would later have become a powerful ally when it came to protecting Irish shipping jobs in 1918. He left Ireland shortly afterwards and did not return until the demise of the company nearly ten years later.

A journal was kept for each of the *Provinces*. This was similar to a ship's log. In these journals, the ships' captains meticulously entered their vessels' operating and navigating procedures, e.g., the time the vessel passed lights such as the Kish. They also entered the numbers of passengers, baggage, parcels and mail sacks. If the mail was delayed in any way, the reason and length of the delay was recorded. This was done so that the financial penalties which could accrue for late mails were not mistakenly appropriated. All manner of entries and descriptions of delays appear in these journals, such as, 'awaiting the arrival of the mail train' or the 'mail vans', or ' loading luggage' and so on. All of these detailed records survive today in excellent condition and are held in the National Library in Kildare Street, Dublin.

The cross channel delivery of mail and passengers by the Provinces continued without any major incident until the outbreak of the First World War and, notwithstanding the hostilities, there was no immediate or significant affect on their operations. The first alarm bells rang in company headquarters in 1917. Less than a year earlier, the Ministry of Shipping had cast its eye on the *Connaught*, which coincidentally had been the fastest in trials. It was requisitioned for 'trooping' in the English Channel and it was so doing when it was torpedoed and lost on 3 March 1917. The Admiralty had at the time of requisitioning promised, 'to be responsible for the consequences of the *Connaught*', but the words proved to be empty. The trooping services of both the *Ulster* and *Munster* were also required by the Admiralty later in 1917.

The loss of the *Connaught* left the company with only three of these vessels, and although the service continued, the Admiralty had ultimate control of the mail boats. This they clearly demonstrated in 1915, when, much to the annoyance of the company's directors, the *Provinces* were ordered into Laird's without prior consultation for the fitting of guns. The viability of the service was put at risk but despite the additional pressure on the three vessels they carried on and 'delivered the goods'.

Despite the company's gallant efforts, there was no escaping the effects the U-boats were having upon shipping in the Irish Sea during 1917. This is also borne out by many descriptive entries in the *Provinces'* journals of sightings and encounters with U-boats. These encounters were not just by chance. German U-Boat commanders were coming right around the British Isles with orders to attack the mail steamers. Why? The answer is simple. They were engaged in important war activity. The number of troops moving between Ireland and England was growing, and many of these were being transported aboard the mail steamers quite separately from any 'trooping' by the *Provinces*. Travelling more and more by this better class of crossing were the very high ranking officers of both the USA and Great Britain.

When the USA entered the War, it established a number and variety of bases around Ireland. This naturally resulted in the movement of thousands of personnel and material to and from these bases. Some of the traffic was via Rosslare - Pembroke but the majority was between Kingstown and Holyhead. This was due to the risk which may not seem so obvious but was greater anywhere in the vicinity of the George's or Bristol Channels. It was not until mid-1917 that there was sufficient numbers of troops travelling on the mail steamers to cause delays and warrant recording in the journals. Before this, the movement of troops to and fro on the mail steamers could be considered as harmless comings and goings of a few troops on leave.

After July 1917 the number of troops travelling aboard the mail steamers grew steadily, as did the escorts that they required. Again, the journals clearly show the loss of time that was accruing due to the increased military activity. The reasons that are recorded are as many as they are varied, such as 'awaiting Admiralty instructions', 'steering zig zag course', 'embarking and disembarking troops', 'awaiting escorts' and many others.

As a matter of policy, escorts were never supplied for the mail steamers in any structured way, but only at the discretion of the Admiralty. These discretionary escorts were provided on occasions of intense troop movement, such as those during December 1917 and January 1918, or when important Admirals such as Sims or figures such as the First Sea Lord and Franklin D. Roosevelt (later President of the USA) were on board. (Roosevelt crossed on 24 July, 1918, to visit Queenstown.) On such occasions, the 'through' journey from London to Queenstown included a night sailing with excellent bar and saloon facilities followed by a splendid breakfast on the train journey to Queenstown. This might also have been the case on the anniversary of the US destroyers reaching Queenstown, when the First Sea Lord and an entourage of high ranking officers crossed in May 1918. Prior to these occasions, there was extensive patrolling and the crossings themselves were very heavily escorted.

In time the number of escorts not only grew but formalised. The procedures and vessels varied in type and arrangement, giving as much cover by sea and air as possible. The escorts were made up of destroyers from both the USA and Britain, seaplanes from the USNAS base at North Wexford, and RAF airships operating between South Wexford and Malahide Castle and those from the main base

NIGHT SERVICE.

JOURNAL kept on board the *Leinster* — Royal Mail Steam Packet.

From HOLYHEAD to KINGSTOWN 16 of *July* 1918

Tuesday	Time A.M.	Wind and Weather.	REMARKS.		
Mail Train arrived on Jetty at	3.13	Light variable winds	Total No. of Irish Mail Bags received		418
Passengers' Luggage & Mails all on Board at	3.33		Total No. of Foreign do.		
Packet Started at	3.34	Rain fog & haze	Total No. of Parcel Post Baskets		
Packet Abreast Breakwater Light at	3.40	at intervals	Minutes delay from Storm		
Passed the Kish at	6.16	varying in	— do. do. Snow		
Packet Abreast Kingstown Light-house (between Pier Heads) at	6.51	density from	31 do. do. Fog		
Time occupied on the Passage of Channel	Hours 3	Minutes 11	— do. do. Collision and to avoid Collision or save life		
Packet at Kingstown Jetty	6.51	Bkwater to arrival	— do. do. Heavy, Foreign or Colonial Mails		
Communication by gangway established at	6.58	Speed reduced	12 do. do. embarking & disembarking		
Mails Landed and in Vans at	7.30	Whistle sounded	U.S.N stores		
Time occupied from arrival of Train on Holyhead Jetty to placing of Mails in Vans at Kingstown	Hours 4	Minutes 17	5. Post office not ready on arrival		
Luggage, &c., Landed at	7.45	Smooth sea	N. Flood from Kish		

1st Class Passengers, 117

2nd do. do.

3rd do. do. 536½

651½

Signed, _____

From KINGSTOWN to HOLYHEAD 15 of *July* 1918

Monday	Time P.M.	Wind and Weather.	REMARKS.		
Mail Train arrived on Jetty at	7.51	Light variable winds	Total No. of Irish Mail Bags received		160
Passengers' Luggage & Mails all on Board at	8.8		Total No. of Foreign do.		
Packet Started at	8.9		Total No. of Parcel Post Baskets		129
Packet Abreast Kingstown Light-house (between Pier Heads) at	8.12	Clear with rain	Minutes delay from Storm		
Passed the Kish at	8.38	Smooth sea	— do. do. Snow		
Packet Abreast Breakwater Light at	11.6		— do. do. Fog		
Time occupied on the Passage of Channel	Hours 2	Minutes 54	— do. do. Collision and to avoid Collision or save life		
Arrived at East end of Holyhead Jetty at	11.13		— do. do. Heavy, Foreign or Colonial Mails		
Communication by gangway established at	11.15		— do. do. Parcel Post		
Mails Landed and in Vans at	11.39		14 do. do. Zig Zag courses		
Time occupied from arrival of Train on Kingstown Jetty to placing of Mails in Vans at Holyhead Jetty	Hours 3	Minutes 48			
Luggage, &c., Landed at	11.54				

1st Class Passengers, 138

2nd do. do.

3rd do. do. 513½

651½

Signed, _____

An extract from the journal of the Leinster

at Anglesey. There were a total of five airship stations with twenty-four machines operating cover for the Irish Sea. The airships that accompanied the mail steamers and troop convoys across the Irish Sea were of the type *SSZ*, which meant Submarine Scout Zero (class). They were armed with a machine gun and a couple of 100 lb bombs. The small gondola suspended beneath the airship had three crew - the mechanic, the wireless operator and navigator. These airships were also said to be capable of detecting submarines by a sonar device lowered from the gondola (if this detection device was to work, conditions would have to be most agreeable). This method of escort was only of assistance during daylight and good weather and was not responsible for any significant number of U-boat losses. The airships operated from the main base at Wales with a maximum flying time of seven hours. This meant that after accompanying a convoy from Wales they had to land in Ireland. Or alternatively, they might operate to their limits and cover as much as 270 miles returning to their original point of departure. Landing facilities in the grounds of Malahide Castle were provided amongst the trees, where even without the nuisance of the trees it took a lot of men to 'haul down the blimp'. Two of the airships regularly seen over Dublin and accompanying the mail ships were *SSZ 34* and *SSZ 35*.

In May 1918, there was heavy reliance on airships for escort duty which was probably prompted by some sensitive crossings. There had also been a large number of U-boat sightings and encounters which had proved fatal for shipping on several occasions. Some of the sightings recorded in the *Leinster's* journal are as follows (on page 49):

Night sailing, December 27, 1917: Torpedo missed by yards.

Night sailing, March 15, 1918: At 4.41 Stand by. At 4.45 Emergency telegraph on full speed astern to avoid submarine close alongside. (This must have been quite a surprise.)

Night sailing, April 21, 1918: At 4.31. Stopped and reversed to avoid collision with vessel ahead without lights, which turned out to be a submarine. (Another surprise.) At 4.33. Emergency telegraph put on full speed ahead.

Day sailing, August 14, 1918: Spotted submarine on port bow 3 miles away.

(The incident of 27 December 1917 was an extremely fortunate escape by the *Leinster*. It was *U-100* which made this attack and was disadvantaged in that it was only able to use one torpedo tube as the others were jammed with debris. It later surfaced and removed the obstruction and then sunk the Tedcacstle's ship *Adela* out of Dublin the same day. The only survivor of the twenty-five aboard this ship was its skipper, Michael Tyrell.)

Worries of this nature were not just confined to the *Leinster* but were a daily operational hazard for the remaining three mail steamers, and indeed all ships that sailed the Irish Sea. The *Ulster* was attacked by torpedo in March and April and the *Munster* was attacked by torpedo in April 1918, all of which missed. There were many other incidents of time lost and delayed sailings, due in part to vessels having to 'stand to, awaiting Admiralty instructions'. This was common when one of the

The top two photographs are of the Leinster *in camouflague and the bottom illustration is an Admiralty First World War Flower Class Sloop. It can be easily seen that one might be confused with the other.*

many convoys was passing in the Irish Sea en route to or from Northern ports. The growing delays also reflected the frequency and huge growth in military and naval traffic.

In March and April 1917, U-boat attack figures reached a climax. The scale of losses off the South West coast of Ireland were horrific as were the growing losses in the Irish Sea. There were extensive U-boat encounters in the Irish Sea during 1917. Captain Newton of the Ulster recorded this very curious reason for a delay during a crossing from Kingstown to Holyhead:

24 March

At **10.30 a.m.:** Slowed and stopped to pick up 3 boats crews which would not take our assistance.
At **10.36 a.m.:** Proceeded at <u>full speed.</u>

Although the sea was 'smooth with light variable winds', it seems inconceivable under normal circumstances that lifeboats adrift in the middle of the Irish Sea would refuse help. However, Captain Newton did not delay but sped off after only six minutes. These men in the open boats may have been the crew from the sailing vessel *Howe* which was captured by a U-boat 4 miles north-east of the *North Arklow Light Vessel* on the same day and put adrift while their vessel was sunk with bombs.

It was not only the British who employed the tactic of decoy ships - it is said to have begun with German vessels. Maybe it was with this in mind that Captain Newton took some added precautions six months later. On this occasion, shortly after significant convoy activity in the Irish Sea, in practically the exact same position and at approximately the same time as the incident on 24 March, very similar circumstances arose again:

13 October

At **10.50 a.m.:** Sighted ship's boat capsized with four men on it. Circled round same until patrol boat came to pick them up.

At **11.04 a.m.:** Proceeded full speed.

This time the delay had taken fourteen minutes, after which time the men adrift on the lifeboat were rescued. These survivors may have been from the *Guinness ship W. M. Barkley* which had been torpedoed seven miles east of the *Kish Light Vessel* with the loss of the captain and four of her crew the previous day. It is claimed that the rescuing vessel was the *HMS Helga* but, if this were true, it only rescued four persons and, mysteriously, these were landed at Newport, Monmouthshire. Another four were picked up by *SS Donnet Head* three miles from Dublin. Following the sinking of their ship, the crew of the *Barkley* were questioned and then given directions for Dublin by the commander of the attacking sub *U-75*.

Airships patrolling the Irish Sea. Above is the Z33 over Malahide and below it is escorting a ship in tow

By September 1918, large amounts of officers and troops could be seen on the mail steamers, the bulk of whom travelled from Kingstown to Holyhead. This activity did not go unnoticed by the Germans who were reported to have had many spies at ports and railheads. This suspicion was supported by several attacks against shore targets on both sides of the Irish Sea which could only have been made with a supply of local intelligence. It was not the least unusual for sailings and disembarkations to be delayed because of routine document and identification checks. Such was the concern of the authorities in this matter that two days after the loss of the *Leinster*, a young English student of geology was arrested for sketching on Killiney beach, Co. Dublin. When he was apprehended by a constable he was reported to have said to him: 'Do you take me for being a spy? I suppose you have to be exact now, owing to the *Leinster* going down.' Funny, you may think, but when the lad appeared before the judge and was later remanded in custody on further charges, he was told: 'six months or join the army.'

It can be difficult to understand how German spies could operate under the noses of the military authorities on an island in the remote north-western extremity of Europe. It must be remembered that although Europe was at war, commerce and trade continued. Such countries as Norway had been neutral and continued to sail ships commercially throughout the world. (The gunrunning ship Aud was disguised as a neutral Norwegian steamer in 1916.) So, for instance, if a ship sailed from South America it might, and often did, have reason to call at Ireland's south-western ports en route to Europe. Not all ships' captains were scrupulous in their examination of crews' papers, and quite often German and Austrian nationals were illegally secreted amongst the crew to spy on the military activities of the Allies. These activities, and the authorities' fear of them, is quite clearly demonstrated in the following and quite unique way. In the Maritime Museum Library, there is a rare 'Office Book' which was kept by the Chief Preventive Officer at Cork during some of the war years. The following are some examples of the revealing entries contained in it:

A letter to The Collector, Custom House, Queenstown, 12.8.1914

To The Collector,

I beg to report that Wilhelm Robert, German subject seaman on board the Norwegian ship 'Sternd' has been landed in Queenstown and taken into custody by the Royal Irish Constabulary.

Oscar Schmidt and Karl Von Wedel, German subjects seamen on board the Norwegian ship *'Pax'* have been landed same time and taken into custody under the same escort.

J. P. Kelly C.P.O.

Copy of Confidential No. A17, 26.12.1914 from the South Irish Coast Defence

Dear Mr Pritchard,

The Cork Police arrested a young German aged 23 named Walter Truppel on the *'Ventura de Larranaga'* on the 24 th.inst.

She had been berthed in Cork since the 22 nd.inst. Do you people keep a keen look out for those enemy seamen on a ship's arrival as it does not seem a good thing to have Germans left aboard berthed ships.

This arrest was made on 'private information'. Would you kindly let me know for the confirmation of G.O.C. what arrangements there are for detecting and detaining these men as far as your authorities are concerned.

Yours Faithfully

T. W. Dickie Captain. T.O. (Or I.O.)

The Chief Preventive Officer replied on the 31.12.1914 to the above thus:

Sir,

I beg to report with reference to the attached letter that the precautions taken are as follows.

The vessel is boarded immediately on arrival, master questioned as to the Nationality of the crew, ship's articles examined and compared.

Vessel rummaged and crew carefully scrutinised for a suspicious 'Enemy'.

Master served with notice not to allow aliens on shore.

Vessel boarded and visited daily.

Police informed of any suspicious enemy.

J. P. Kelly

The above reply was a working copy of the original and the second last sentence was amended to read: 'Vessel boarded during working hours and occasionally when silent' ('not busy' to be presumed).

It is clear from these entries that the authorities were unhappy with the thoroughness of the inspections carried out, and in the absence of any denial by Mr Kelly in his economic reply, confirmation of this may be inferred. Mr Kelly may have had good reason to feel somewhat aggrieved as the Customs department was badly in need of staff and out-of-pocket expenses for travelling inspections throughout the region (from Fenit to Youghal) were often hard to reclaim.

The Yanks also had had problems with spies at ports and railheads and further confirmation of this is gleaned from the diary letters of US Chief Petty Officer John O'Brien to his wife back home in America. The contents of some of these letters were published in the *Wexford People* 12 December, 1978. Whilst operating as an intelligence officer and based in the Naval Air Station at Wexford, he recorded this diary entry on 28 September, 1918: 'Went to dance at Rosslare to investigate German spy'.

His letters back home were also able to add weight to the suspicion that more than one submarine was operating in the vicinity of the Irish Sea at the time of the attack on the *Leinster*. He further noted on 5 October: 'Rain today. No flying and four subs reported in our area'. And on 6 October: 'We are rushed with messages from planes and reports of subs'.

It was clear, given the very large numbers of military personnel involved, that these steamers had become involved in what can only be described as troop carrying and that the risk to the vessels and the travelling public had increased considerably. The Germans were well aware of this activity and, as stated earlier, U-boats were ordered to attack these ships. This is demonstrated clearly by the following record of an encounter in the George's Channel on 25 April, 1918 (it is quite likely that this was the same submarine that was encountered by the *Leinster* on 21 April.). On 23 April, the American destroyer *Cushing* successfully damaged a U-boat but could not confirm the 'kill'. Later, on 25 April, the sloop *Jasmine* from Queenstown, Cork located the surfaced U-boat and sank it with depth charges after it dived. This was *U-104*, and following the explosion there was a huge gush of rising air from which the only survivor was recovered. This was Karl Eschenber, aged just twenty-two years, and he related the following story: 'Our craft left Heligoland and came via Scotland down the West and South West coast of Ireland into the Irish Sea, where we made two unsuccessful attempts to torpedo the Holyhead-Kingstown mail steamers'.

If the interrogation was transcribed accurately, the questions arising are obvious. How did they know they were the mail boats? How did they know they were travelling to Kingstown? It was known that the German U-boats were not only out to get these mail boats, but in particular to get the *Leinster*. But why the *Leinster*?

Returning again to the journals of the mail steamers, and another of the company's volumes - *The Workings of the Irish Mail Service from Heuston - Dun Laoghaire,* these next few entries make it quite clear why the German U-boat commanders took great risks hanging about in the Irish Sea for a shot at these plum targets. We know now that their persistence paid off on 10 October, 1918 with fatal results for both the victim and the attacker:

1917

28 December: Embarking military equipment.

1918

13 March: Embarking military.

22 March: Escorted by American destroyer *92-Gridley.*

24 April: Embarking naval luggage.

7 May: Escorted by airships *SSZ 34* and *35.*

22 May: Embarking naval luggage.

1 July: Embarking military.

16 July: Landing and loading naval stores in mail train for Queenstown.

23 July: Landing and loading naval stores in mail train for Queenstown.

27 July: Embarking US naval luggage.

18 September: 400 Military shut out. [Passage refused.]

19 September: 320 Military shut out.

The entries above are only samples and are repeated consistently throughout the war years. Remember that these were reasons why delays occurred. In the case of 'luggage', it was obviously not the hand luggage of civilian passengers which caused the delays.

Shutting out

The records of the *Leinster's* last few months of service are noteworthy, as they indicate why so many were *'shut out'* (i.e. not allowed to board) and raise some questions which are not so easily answered. Up until February 1918, the numbers of passengers travelling were in the low hundreds, after which they began to escalate during the restoration of night sailings. 'Shutting out' began on 9 September (eleven days before commander Ramm set out from Heligoland in *UB-123*) and continued unabated right up until 1 October. It came about because of the large number of civilians and military personnel unable to gain passage on the

Ulster, which had uncharacteristically been out of service for a full five weeks. Although large numbers were left behind, the *Leinster* 'shut out' at exactly 650 passengers. This had not always been the case with the *Leinster*, nor the other packets as they quite often exceeded 700 passengers and continued to do so. But not the *Leinster* in 1918. Why not? She had originally been licensed for 1,400; this was reduced to 1,100 and the number of lifeboats increased from six to ten. Even with 100 crew, the total number carried never approached the licensed figure. Was it because of additional baggage of some kind or space allocated for additional stores that the company would refuse passage to thousands of fare-paying travellers?

The mail packet was also the preferred crossing of the landed gentry, noble people, officers and all manner of politicians and celebrities. The mail boat sailings were particularly popular with Irish MPs - they not only warmed to the comforts provided by the crossing but desired to be seen to support an Irish company and Irish jobs. It was also a convenience which Irish MPs enjoyed free of charge as a reward for the support they gave to the CDSPCo. and the influence which they exerted to reverse the earlier granting of the mail contact to the LNWR. The mail crossing was not only seen as the safest and fastest but also the most fashionable means of crossing. It was, in effect, a snobbish way to travel.

The importance of the connection to Queenstown, or indeed from Kingstown to any of the major towns in Ireland, has been clearly demonstrated. It can also be seen from the above journal entries that the US presence in Ireland was by then well-established. It must also be stated that normal 'troop transport' was aboard LNWR trains and boats. They frequently put on 'specials' to and from the ports and with what must have been 'overspills' going to the mail steamers of the CDSPCo. I say 'overspill' as there were only a small number of 'specials' mentioned in relation to the mail steamers, but obviously quite large numbers of troops travelled. As the LNWR had the main contract with the government for the movement of troops, it was left to the CDSPCo. to recover any moneys due to it from them. This later became a problem.

The mail boats carried troops. The company was aware of it! The Ministry of Shipping and the Admiralty were aware of it! The captains and crew were aware of it! U-boats were aware of it! They all knew that the mail steamers were under constant threat and escaped by the 'skin of their teeth' on many occasions. The company did all in its power and persistently petitioned the Admiralty for escorts. But the general public knew nothing! Or did they?

Maybe it was the number of these sailings that took place at night, or the fact that censorship during this period was so thorough, that kept the public ignorant of what was happening. Whether or not they knew, however, it did not matter as there was no other method by which the public could cross the channel, except by sea.

Cargo

During the course of researching this book, I asked the Department of the Navy in the USA what the 'USN. Stores' or 'USN baggage', so often mentioned in the journals, could be. The Department replied: 'it could be possibly anything going to or from any of their bases in Ireland'. This, of course, is an unashamed and perfectly correct reply.

With the exception of urgent cases, as in the earlier 90 tons of munitions transported aboard the Ulster, the mail boats were probably not suitable for the transportation of 'war material' in the normal understanding of the term. It was, of course, possible to carry specialised items in some quantity. A further inter-pretation of 'military equipment' may lie in Rathmines, Dublin. At the end of Observatory Lane, off the Lower Rathmines Road, was the firm of Howard Grubb and Company Ltd. This firm excelled in, and gained a world wide reputation in the manufacture of optical lenses for telescopes. It was responsible for the construction of the largest telescope in the world at the time - the Great Vienna Telescope - and many others. More to the point, Grubb had pioneered development of the periscope, and during the war, the factory at Dublin became extremely important and principally relied upon for the provision of optical lenses for Allied periscopes. The tubes for these were manufactured by Vickers at Barrow-in-Furness and then shipped to Rathmines for the fitting of the lenses. When finally completed, the periscope measured thirty-six feet, weighed twelve hundredweight and could with-stand pressure of 150 pounds per square inch. It was then shipped back to Britain for fitting at a naval port. Although there was a guard placed around Grubb's works at Rathmines, it was the sea journeys that were considered to be most risky. So valuable were these cargoes that they were shipped only one per sailing. With Dublin still supplying the lenses, the assembly of periscopes, rangefinders, gun sights and so on was eventually shifted from Rathmines to St Albans and continued there until 1920. (Eventually Howard Grubb and Co. of Dublin and St Albans was purchased by Parsons of Newcastle upon Tyne to form Sir Howard Grubb, Parsons and Company.)

There are many stories still in circulation about possible clandestine cargoes that the *Provinces* are supposed to have carried, but as yet these are unsub-stantiated. The specialised items produced by Grubb are a real possibility - but only that.

Captain Birch

In command of the *Leinster* in 1918 was Captain William Birch. Within the company he held the fleet senior title of Commodore. He was indeed a fine sailor and many of his passengers had great respect for him. They often shared jovial conversation with him on the bridge during crossings. Although Captain Birch began his training in sailing vessels, his early surroundings and upbringing were most unlikely for a sailor-to-be. His grandfather, William, appears to have been a rope merchant in the early nineteenth century. Whilst residing in the heart of commercial Dublin at 21 College Green, his father Edwin, who was described as a 'woollen merchant' and 'gentleman' met Eliza Worn. Eliza was a hairdresser in the family business at 17 Dawson Street. This establishment was described as 'Worn's Perfumerers and Hairdressers', claiming patronage of the Lord Lieutenant and several members of the Royalty. At the junction of number 17 was 1-3 Molesworth Street where the family seems to have partly resided and where Eliza and Edwin met. They were married on 14 March, 1848 in their notable parish Church of St

Anne's, situated on the opposite corner. They lived in several apartments at various addresses in the fashionable inner Dublin City and, it seems, it may have been the interaction with merchants and shipowners that sparked William Birch's interest in the sea.

The couple had two sons, Charles and William. William was born in 1857 while they were still at Molesworth Street, Dublin. Without extensive searching, little more could be added about William's career that was not included in the fine tribute later paid to him in the Holyhead *Chronicle* in the issue of 18 October 1918. Although Captain Birch was born in Dublin and was 'Irish to the core', he settled in Holyhead and he was their man:

Captain Birch, who was in command of the RMS Leinster, began his career and served his time in sailing ships. Part of his time was spent on board the Singapore of the White Star Line. Later he became mate of the notorious barge Emulation, of which he was wont to tell many interesting stories. After leaving this vessel he joined the Pacific Steam Navigation Company's coasting steamer May Pocha, but did not remain long in that company, for having married in the meantime, Captain Birch decided to remain in home waters. Shortly after this he became an officer with the Dublin Steam Packet Company and soon rose to be master on the Liverpool route. From there he changed to the Holyhead-Kingstown mail service, a course with which he was well acquainted. Captain Birch was a well known and interesting personality, and his loss will be greatly regretted by those who trusted themselves in his hands during the anxious periods of submarine activity. His numerous friends will be interested to know that he received promotion in connection with the incident of the sinking of the Kish Lightship close to which he ended his brilliant career, dying at his post for his country, like a true son of Albion.

(Reference to the *Kish Lightship* concerns the time the *Leinster* rammed and sunk the *Albatross* on 8 September, 1902, during thick fog. The lives of all the light-keepers were saved and the vessel, valued in excess of £30,000, was subsequently refloated.)

Captain Birch received his mate's ticket at the age of twenty-four and immediately made a name for himself as a leader of men. There were many stories of remarkable improvisation /during long voyages and uncomfortable con-frontations with disagreeable shipmates aboard the *Emulation*. A story which sticks is the remarkably similar one to that of *Hemmingway's Old Man Of The Sea*. In this the young Birch, who had a keen interest in shark fishing, had occasion to row after one whilst fishing from his ship off the west coast of America. After baiting a lump of pork, a large shark found it irresistible and ran with it until the line broke. Without hesitation William Birch hopped into a leaky punt and pursued the great fish. After a long struggle, he regained the end of the line and managed to tow the shark for some distance. Unable to regain the ship and refusing to give up the catch, his shipmates brought the ship around and returned to pick him up. He then got his mates to pass him a harpoon with which he finished the job and retrieved the huge fish on board the ship.

One of the Provinces belching black smoke leaving Kingstown

PUBLIC NOTICE.
PASSENGERS
LEAVING IRELAND

I, GENERAL SIR JOHN GRENFELL MAXWELL, K.C.B., K.C.M.G., C.V.O., D.S.O., Commanding in Chief His Majesty's Forces in Ireland, hereby Order that no person shall embark as a passenger on board any vessel except at one of the following ports, viz: Dublin (North Wall), Kingstown, Belfast, and Greenore. Each passenger must produce satisfactory credentials or proofs of identity to the Military Embarkation Officer or Police Authorities at the place of intended embarkation and give valid reasons for the intended journey.

J. G. MAXWELL,
GENERAL,
COMMANDING-IN-CHIEF,
THE FORCES IN IRELAND.

HEADQUARTERS, IRISH COMMAND.
2nd May, 1916.

This public notice confirms the authorities' fears about the movements of non-nationals (German spies) within the UK

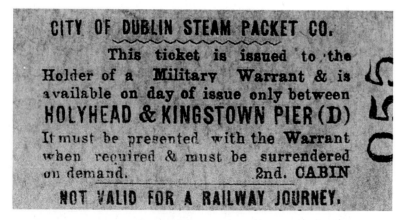

The boat ticket confirms that the military were afforded travel concessions aboard the mailboats

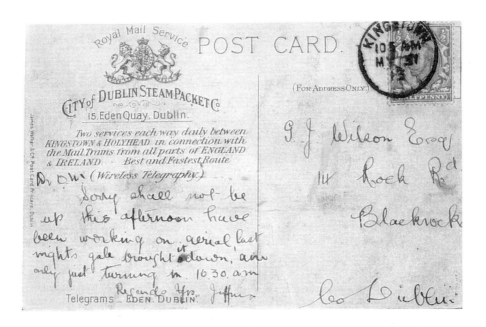

A postcard of the Connaught posted in Kingstown by the radio officer A. Jeffries who later lost his life on the Leinster. *Interestingly he expected same day delivery*

Dangerous crossings

Let there be no doubt as to the risks involved crossing the Irish Sea during that summer and autumn. The War's end was approaching but the scale of German U-boat activity in the Irish Channel was staggering. The earlier diagram of U-boat attacks clearly demonstrates a change in emphasis and the vigorous determination on the part of the U-boats in the Irish Sea during the latter stages of the war. As shown later, there is a diary of U-boat encounters for October 1918 which shows that although an end to the war was imminent, attacks were still frequent. The extent of the involvement of Ireland in this War has probably not been made sufficiently clear, nor is it appreciated by Irish citizens, who tend to think only of the young recruits that Ireland sent to foreign parts.

Prior to, and during, the early years of the War, Irish manufacturers made repeated petitions for government contracts. As raw materials for industry were rigorously controlled and supplied only to those who contributed to the War, such contracts were essential for the survival of engineering and manufacturing industries. With the exception of just a few private munitions manufacturers, Ireland was passed over in the awarding of such contracts. Persistent petitioning for this work was rebuffed and the response by British officials to agitation by the All-Ireland Munitions and Government Supplies Committee was summed up in this derogatory reply: 'They could as easily eat shells as manufacture them'. This wary and dogged refusal to give Ireland any opportunity to produce munitions existed during a crucial period of shortages in the industry. The Secretary of State for War, Lord Kitchener, had already been in conflict with Lloyd George and Churchill over the same shortages.

This allusion to Ireland's industrial incompetence has a strange twist of irony to it. Not only was Ireland able to produce quality munitions but it was responsible for keeping the population of Britain from starvation. The Department of Agri-culture and Technical Instruction for Ireland was able to show, in 1918, that imported food stuffs from a wide range of countries into Britain was topped by that of Ireland and was exceeded only late in the War by the USA - and that was only as a result of the imposed import restrictions on feeding stuffs into Ireland. Beef, pork and mutton shipped across the Irish Sea amounted to nearly 40% of Britain's consumption.

Repeated pressure eventually won a survey commissioned by Lloyd George in 1916 and the results were clearly in favour of utilising Irish manufacturing capabilities to the full. As a result, National Shell Factories were erected in Waterford, Cork and Galway, and the existing one in Dublin was enlarged. The full production capabilities of these units were severely hampered initially by bad management (not Irish) and poor quality. This was improved but not until early 1918 was efficient and high quality production attained. Despite high performances in production quality and competitive cost output, contracts were continually in jeopardy. The fates of these factories were in similar hands to those that eventually brought down the CDSPCo. Petitions from British industrialists for the redirection of Irish contracts were constantly arriving at Whitehall. When the War ended and the munitions factories closed, most of the machinery found its way back to main-land Britain. Other military production facilities were situated at Arklow, Co. Wicklow; bomb parts at Inchicore Railway Works; aircraft works at Sir John Rogersons Quay and Portobello, Dublin, and, as already mentioned, Grubb of Rathmines.

The Kynoch's Munitions Works at Arklow suffered extensive damage and many fatalities during the night of 21 September, 1917 when it blew up. It is still said by many local people that it was shelled by a German submarine. This may seem to be an exaggeration, but there are many aspects to the disaster that remain mysterious - for example, the subsequent testimonies that three blasts and 'whooshes' were heard before the main explosion and the mysterious car with bright lights directed at the sea from above the works. There were several other equally unexplained accounts from other credible witnesses. It was not at all unusual for a submarine to shell shore targets; Scarborough had been bombed in such a fashion just two weeks earlier. In addition, there was at least one earlier sighting of a U-boat near Cahore. This was a little unusual in that it was daytime and, generally speaking, U-boats did not operate inside of the Arklow Banks where this one was quite certainly spotted when it surfaced. Further confirmation of the almost matter-of-fact way that U-boat commanders might attack shore based targets is obtained from the log of *U-100*. If accurately translated, the intention of Captain von Loe of U-100 after sinking Tedcastle's *Adela off* Holyhead on 27 December, 1917 was this: 'I take to the South of Ireland, hoping to be able to fire during the night at the South coast.'

In 1958, salvors working at the wreck of the *Anna Troop* on the Arklow Bank are said to have encountered the wreck of a submarine but there is no record of a German submarine missing in these waters at that time.

Captain Birch was at all times aware of the dangers and nuances of the Holyhead-Kingstown route, to the extent that only a few months prior to the loss of the *Leinster*, he had accompanied Captain T.B. Williams in his airship during a convoy protection flight across the Irish Sea. It was indeed a great tribute to the masters of these remaining mail steamers that they eluded for so long the constant and dogged attempts by the German U-boat commanders to sink them. Nevertheless, Captain Birch knew that the odds must have been stacked against him. He had escaped attack for so long and he confided in his fellow officers that he 'knew his luck would run out'.

Despite renegotiating the contract for the delivery of the mails in August 1918 for the reduced sum of £78,000, with a six month opt out clause, it had become increasingly difficult to operate the service to the tight schedules required. Petitions to the Admiralty for escorts continued, as did exasperation with the Ministry for Shipping for not providing the priority nor the wherewithal for replacement of the lost *Connaught*. Although the remaining mail boats had avoided being requi-sitioned (indeed why should they have been, when they were quite efficiently moving troops with them in any event), many of the company's other vessels did not. Compounding their problems with the loss of the *Leinster*, the CDSPCo. was left with only two vessels with which to operate the service. This was, of course, insufficient and necessitated the expensive chartering of additional vessels.

When finally the *Munster* sailed out of Kingstown in November 1920, she was accompanied by her remaining sister vessel, the *Ulster*. The *Ulster* was captained by the promoted and surviving first officer of the *Leinster*, Mr Patrick Crangle. It was the final crossing for these magnificent vessels from which they never returned. Patrick's surviving son Edward has fond memories of holidays aboard the mail boats, and he remembers the officers 'dressing up' for their ironic and final farewell to the remaining *Provinces* before they sailed to an ignominious end in a German breakers' yard.

The end of the City of Dublin Steam Packet Company

The company no longer found itself in a position to compete with its old rival, the LNWR, which had continued to operate from the Liffey. The LNWR was expecting new vessels in 1919 and it finally won the mail contract from the CDSPCo. The LNWR had not come through the war totally unscathed either. In 1916, it lost *Connemara* and in 1918, the *Sliebhbloom*, both by collision. Despite these losses, the LNWR ultimately won out and secured the remaining cross channel leg of the contract. This completed the 'straight through' delivery contract for the mails, coveted for so long by this company.

Notwithstanding its success and its contribution to the demise of the CDSPCo., it was unrelenting. During the 'overspill' of troops onto the mail steamers, the CDSPCo. found it difficult to recoup its fare receipts from the LNWR with whom the Ministry of Defence had the contract for their movement. The CDSPCo. later spent many argumentative sessions in the courts over moneys due to them.

This was the end of the City of Dublin Steam Packet Co. and over a century of cross channel history, seventy years of which involved transporting the mails. Although it was a competitive and efficient company, maintaining the highest standards, it was wound up by a select committee of the House of Lords in 1922 and liquidated in 1930. The workings of the company were swallowed up by the British and Irish Steamship Company: 'All is fair in love and war' (and in business, some might add).

Chapter 4
UB-123

UB-123 was one of the last submarines to come from the German shipbuilders before the end of the War. She belonged to the UB 111 class of submarine and was commissioned from the Bremen yards on 6 March 1918. There were essentially three classes of German submarines. Firstly, the 'U' class which were the largest and were extremely well built vessels with extended range capacity. This class was ultimately designed to an incredible size of 3,000 tons and provided comfortable conditions for cruises that could last as long as three months. These large 'cruiser' type of submarines had a range of 3,000 miles and travelled across the Atlantic to attack shipping on the East coast of the United States of America. Unusually, a small experimental number of them were fitted with broadside torpedo tubes, and some were used to transport valuable cargoes.

Commander Robert Ramm's submarine was like the U-122 shown here

The UB 111 vessels were classed as coastal or 'smaller ocean going' submarines and gained considerable prestige in the U-boat fleet towards the end of the war. German commanders often remarked that this UB class was probably the finest developed and if the shipyards had concentrated on constructing this class rather than the more expensive and longer-to-build U class, it might have altered the outcome of the war. The later UB class displaced between 600-700 tons and were very stoutly built vessels. They had four forward torpedo tubes and one stern tube which accommodated 20 inch torpedoes in quarters that were said to be cramped. Each had a 4.1 inch (22 pounder) deck gun, a machine gun and excellent wireless facilities. A distinct difference associated with UB-123 was that not only had it got a forward deck gun but also an aft one. (This second gun, although out of context with the familiar specifications for these vessels, was quite definitely referred to by Commander Ramm.) This fact later becomes of importance when a submarine is sighted surfaced in the Irish Sea after the attack on the *Dundalk*. *UB-123* was also fitted with the latest 'sound aerial' listening device. Submerged UB vessels achieved 7.5 knots and on the surface these 180 foot vessels cruised at an average speed of 10 knots, but they could sustain 14 knots for long periods. Lastly, there was the UC class which was a mine laying submarine. It was akin to the UB class with several torpedoes which could be used before or after jettisoning its cargo of mines.

The photo of *UB-122*, which was identical to *UB-123*, with its long range radio antennae erected. The more familiar shorter range aerial which extended from stem to stern across the conning tower could be used immediately upon surfacing.

This class of submarine would appear to be extremely modern to the untrained eye, and it is hard to believe that this photograph was taken over eighty years ago. In many ways the developments during the First World War were almost surreal in their contrasts. For instance, on land, albeit the last of its kind, there was a mounted cavalry charge against field artillery. But there was also the most horrible ability to wage chemical and germ warfare. In the air there was the use of kites and balloons. But there was also the use of aeroplanes with canvas wings that could launch crude but lethal air to ground rockets. On sea there was the use of sailing vessels and steam trawlers, but also aircraft carriers. Beneath the sea there were sophisticated mines with proximity detonators that were shipped across the Atlantic in huge quantities, assembled and supplied to mine layers at the rate of 2,000 per day. On the other hand, thirty years later, firewood and all manner of basic commodities were being rationed in Ireland. And, of course, the submarines, some of which were laboriously driven by steam, and the technically superior German U-boat which was still in vogue twenty years after the war. Effectively these scenes were the transformation of the obsolete and labour intensive modes of war to more advanced mechanisation which was aided by the technical innovations of mass production. A huge leap was taking place in the science of waging war and regrettably the improvement in the science of killing continues.

The War soon became one which the British have so often said lacked any semblance of chivalry. Duels, a thing of the past, were fought by submarine chasers and submarine commanders. All kinds of new weapons were being unleashed on battle weary troops and innocent civilians. Wave upon wave of men were ordered to their death 'over the top'. The objective was to win, by almost any means.

In particular, the constant stream of criticism directed at the unchivalrous U-boat skippers, not totally unwarranted, represented an unreadiness and a complete misreading of the development of the submarine and its capacity to influence an outcome to the War. The German U-boat campaign was an extremely narrow but well focused operation. Its object was to sink merchant shipping to the extent that the Allies would be starved of all the ships, supplies and merchant seamen they needed to win the War and, ultimately, the ability to survive. The German U-boat commanders were under orders not to unnecessarily engage warships in duels that they could lose, but to divert them here and there, and to overstretch them wherever possible. For whatever reason, in the latter stages of the First World War, the U-boats showed a marked reluctance to confront Allied warships.

A First World War submarine torpedoes a merchant ship

Robert Ramm

Robert Ramm entered the Naval service as a cadet at the age of nineteen. He completed the routine non-commissioned training aboard *SMS Hessen* before he entered submarine school in April 1916. He later served on submarines U-76 ('Foundered in the North Cape. 32 survivors'), *U-49* ('Rammed in the Bay Of Biscay. No survivors) and *U-43* ('Survived') until he received command of UB-123 on 6 April 1918 at the age of twenty-seven.

Oberleutnant (Oblt) G. Z. (Junior Officer) Ramm's first voyage in UB-123 began in July 1918, three months after Germany's final attempt to overrun the Allies on the Western Front, and one month before the Allies retaliated with a successful rolling offensive that ultimately won the land war. (The fact that this was also the Americans' first and last major engagement gives an indication of

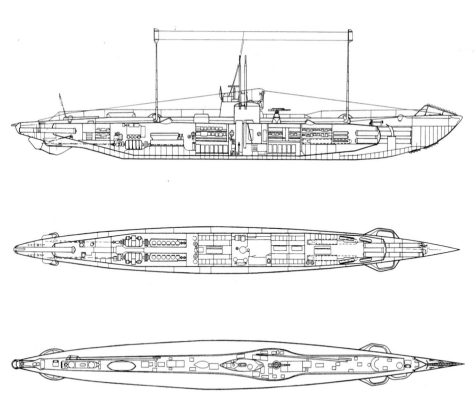

Looking far more modern than from the First World War, in the first photo is a UB 11 class of submarine in rough weather off Heligoland. Below is a UB class of III submarine

how critical their contribution was.) Open revolt in the German army and navy had become apparent and the War became extremely difficult for U-boat commanders. Young Ramm had entered the service as a career officer in training. He had witnessed the brink to which the German High Command had brought the Allies only to see victory slip from their grasp. He had achieved his own command and felt that he was in a position to strike a blow for Germany. Despite his enthusiasm and hope of contributing to a reversal of Germany's fading fortunes, his first voyage proved to be relatively ineffectual. This was to alter significantly for his second, which was also his last.

Photographs of Robert Ramm at different times in his naval career

Although German submarines were nearly as numerous as ever, the tide of events had turned in favour of the Allies. Their powerful and growing net was gathering and had begun to tighten. The Dover barrage was effectively in place. With some exceptions, the Great North Sea Barrage was in place at the Norwegian and Scottish ends and the middle section, designated for completion by the US, was progressing speedily. The Heligoland Bight was also awash with mines laid by both sides and German naval craft were increasingly using the Kiel Canal to enter the Skagerrak in order to gain access to the North Sea.

The three photographs that exist in the U-boat archives at Cuxhaven reveal little about Robert Ramm. The earliest one shows him and his crew having a delicate tea break; it has an air of being carefree. But the other two, and in particular his portrayal in an officer's uniform, show signs of strain and tiredness. The first and last of these photographs are shown.

UB-123: the first voyage

15 July 1918: After delivery of *UB-123* on 6 April, she was assigned to the third U-Boat Flotilla. Tests took unusually long and lasted until 14 July. On 15 July, Commander Robert Ramm and his crew of thirty-five aboard the *UB-123* left Heligoland and sailed for the Skagerrak. If direct entry to the North Sea was to be considered, then extensive preliminary mine clearance would have been necessary. Ramm did in fact leave via the Kiel Canal, where he narrowly avoided collision with incoming *U-70*.

16 July 1918: *UB-123* reached the Skagerrak where it stopped but later released the Swedish steamer *Albatross*. Later in the day, four more neutral merchantmen were halted. Like the Allies, Germany blockaded any suspicious vessels. On this occasion they were the Danish vessels *Constantin, Anin, Nierthholm* and the *Hjortholm*. Suspecting their papers, and with the assistance of UB-120, he put the crew on board and escorted three of them to Swinedemunde, a port on the north-east coast of Germany. Ramm radioed ahead and prepared the authorities to expect the three vessels. However, the ship's papers were found to be in order and the ves-sels were later released. The halting of these vessels would seem to be a minor victory, but not unlike the activities of the Allies, it was necessary to dominate the shipping lanes as far as possible. Nevertheless, Ramm did obtain the important information from the captain of *Constantin* about the 'new English restricted zone in the west'.

17 July 1918: UB-123 continued to operate in the Skagerrak and encountered several problems with compasses, diving and steering equipment. The steering was particularly troublesome and had to be operated from the rear of the submarine. Despite the difficulties which would continue, Ramm set out for the east coast of Scotland.

18 July 1918: After traversing the North Sea, Ramm arrived at the Moray Firth on the east coast of Scotland, where he observed several Allied warships. It was from here that the Great North Sea Barrage was being constructed and the regular comings and goings of cruisers and mine layers with escorting destroyers would have been obvious, presenting opportunities to inflict a lot of damage. Ramm attempted an attack, but the torpedo missed due to 'disadvantaged circumstances'. From a drawing Commander Ramm made, he appears to have sailed submerged through a very heavy convoy and was very lucky to have escaped after making this attack. He did note that he later sailed through some debris and an oily area and speculated that the torpedo might have struck a more distant vessel. Further efforts were made by Ramm to engage the enemy with his deck gun but without success. For his trouble, he was chased by several destroyers to sixty metres and depth charged. (What commander Ramm did not know was that the operations he observed would ultimately seal off his re-entry to the North Sea - and the fate of all on board *UB-123*.)

19 July 1918: Despite the difficulties as a result of the extending North Sea barrage, or as Ramm describes it 'the new English restricted zone', which led some commanders to go right around the Shetlands or even further north, Commander Ramm reckoned on what he termed a 'weak spot'. The Fair Channel between the Shetlands and the Orkneys was still the preferred 'North About' route and it was through here Ramm sailed on 19 July. His passage was not without incident as he reported being scraped by a 'search cable'.

Commander Ramm did not pass through the Minches as was common but came west of the Outer Hebrides. It seems that from this day the occupants of *UB-123* began to feel the effects of their earlier encounter with Allied destroyers. The crew was depleted and debilitated owing to the absence of the sailors who were earlier put aboard the captured steamers and some sickness which had developed amongst the remainder. Cases of infected teeth and gonorrhea were later reported along with the captain's efforts to rest the crew. Ramm remained beset by faulty compasses.

20 July 1918: There is little entered in Ramm's log on this day except that he meets up with *UB-121* and exchanges messages. Although Ramm did not record anything significant for this day, it was a busy day for both the Allies and the other submarines which were in the same area. This was the area situated between Northern Ireland and Scotland and is referred to as the North Channel. Also in this general area at that time were *U-54, UB-64, UB-90, UB-120, UB-121* and *UB-124*. This was a critical area for shipping as the narrowness of the channel with its wide and deep approaches made it a perfect stalking area where U-boats could watch for convoys travelling to or from the large north-western ports. Such was the case of convoy OLX 39, seven vessels outward bound with an unusually heavy escort of twelve warships, that included a destroyer for each vessel. On 19 July, the giant White Star liner Justicia (32,234 tons, requisitioned by the Government for troop transport from the yards at Belfast as Statendam in 1917 and managed by The White Star Line) was sailing in this convoy when she was torpedoed 20 miles west of Skerryvore. Not fatally damaged, she limped on a return journey to port but was attacked again by UB-64. This second attack still did not complete the job and *UB-64* suffered intensive depth charging and damage for her trouble. Having sunk *HMS Anchusa* the day before, U-54 also joined in the attack but the coup de grace was delivered by UB-124 on 20 July (also on her first cruise). She too suffered a terrible hammering by depth charges from the escorting destroyers and had to be abandoned by her inexperienced crew before being scuttled.

Whether or not commander Ramm played any active part with the pack in this attack seems unlikely but a copy of a chart or sketch accompanying his log indicates an 'X' in the same area and the date '20/7'.

21 July 1918: Ramm guides his submarine to the West of St Kilda where he hoped to rendezvous with *UB-90* and *UB-124*. Probably unaware of the recent engagement, his efforts were fruitless. He proceeds south-east to patrol the area earlier observed by *UB-73* and *U-96* as being the area where convoys dispersed.

22 July 1918: Detected by listening devices *UB-123* was attacked by an English destroyer with depth charges and forced to lie low at fifty-five meters. Ramm later surfaced and removed the signal mast and sound-locator which 'rattled a lot underwater'. He then contacted *U-54* which reported good target opportunities at the north edge of Sector I. At this time, it was Ramm's stated intention to contact UB-62 which was on its way to Sector II. The weather remained 'thick' and no further action was reported.

23 July 1918: As advised, Commander Ramm proceeded to position off Barra Head. In his preparations for an attack, he discovered that, added to his difficulties with the steering and the compasses, some of the torpedoes were rendered useless owing to faulty mechanisms.

24 July 1918: Further south-west in the North Channel, *UB-123* was hunted by destroyers, one of which it took a failed shot at. Airships were also on the prowl but he did manage to communicate with *UB-62* during the night.

25 July 1918: At a position 15 miles south-west of Skerryvore, Ramm mistakenly made a surface attack on a destroyer in bad visibility. He immediately dived the boat upon recognition. Sickness in the boat increased which reduced his deep-water 'steerers' to one. He remained underwater to avoid the hunting destroyer.

26 July 1918: Again this day was unrewarding for Ramm. Several vessels were sighted between Fanad Head and Tory Island without any opportunity to strike. Another torpedo was discovered to be faulty.

27 July 1918: Patrolling south-east of Skerryvore without event.

28 July 1918: Patrolling south-west of Skerryvore. Armed steam trawlers were observed on patrol, otherwise no encounters. A further torpedo was found to be faulty.

29 July 1918: While patrolling in the southern entrance to the Minches, Ramm attacked a 2,000 ton steamer without success. He was immediately set upon by patrol boats but avoided the attack by turn of speed. He then encountered his next problem. Broken valve springs on the diesel engines.

30 July 1918: Ramm manoeuvred his boat into the Little Minch and although he encountered some targets, he was forced to extricate himself from the sound. Once more he experienced mechanical difficulties. This time it was with smoke from an overheating transformer and a failed compass light. He rounded Barra and surfaced to air the boat. Another submarine was sighted but failed to respond to the wireless.

31 July 1918: Ramm cruises between Tory Island and the North Channel. No opportunities presented themselves with the exception of signal exchanges with *UB-62* and **UB-91**.

1 August 1918: Events for Ramm on this day were not quite so mundane. After communicating with the commander of *UB-94* just north-west of Tory Island, he positioned for an attack on one of two destroyers without success. Later with Tory Island to the East, Ramm spotted a steamer. A further two steamers followed close behind, all of which passed over his submerged boat. Ramm surfaced to attack from the rear with the boat's two deck guns. After he fired, one of the steamers lowered a boat but the other two turned and steamed down on Ramm at full speed. It was a trap! He quickly dived to fifty meters, followed immediately by depth charging from the buzzing boats above. Twenty-eight depth charges were fired and at sixty-five meters both sets of hydroplanes and lights failed. The boat became 'heavy' and fell in circles to deeper than seventy meters. After three hours at this depth and three to four tons of water having been taken on by the boat, Ramm used his compressed air to lighten the boat and blow out the water. His action was a success and response was again restored to the helms. During his enforced stay on the bottom, he heard several steamers and destroyers pass over in search of his boat. After some time, *UB-123* surfaced again to test her machinery and transmit a warning of the Allied trap which was set for her sister boats. Having had enough, *UB-123* commenced her return to base but only one day earlier than he had scheduled.

2 - 12 August 1918: Commander Ramm sailed again through the Fair Isle Channel but on this occasion kept to the south of the little island. He continued to be dogged by patrol boats and on one occasion had to remain submerged for thirteen hours. Machinery faults continued and a total of sixteen valve springs broke. The boat returned to Wilmshaven through the Skagerrak again. She was followed in by *UB-89* and signed off on 12 August.

This was the end of Oblt Ramm's first voyage in *UB-123*. The cruise lasted twenty-eight days and covered a staggering 4,780 nautical miles with only three hundred of these travelled whilst submerged. At an average of 5-6 knots, this meant only 50-60 hours running time underwater. The vast majority of the journey time was performed on the surface and much of it during daylight hours, submerging only to navigate sensitive areas and to attack. Even at that late stage in the War, submariners would not seem to have been at risk outside the most sensitive areas, which in turn gives credence to the effectiveness of the patrol lane system and blockading as a legitimate and effective method of warfare.

Although this patrol by any wartime standards may seem relatively uncon-frontational, considerable credit is due to Commander Ramm. On his first command of a new boat he took an early initiative with the steamers in the Skagerrak. He used the valuable information he obtained during the seizures and at all times made efforts to communicate relevant information to others. He suffered badly from a boat with deficient machinery, faulty torpedoes and a reduced number of crew. Where a lesser man would have laid low, he continued on station and in pursuit of targets. The log (edited by the author) also demonstrates that it had become extremely difficult for inexperienced U-boat commanders to make suc-cessful attacks without ever increasing risks. Notwithstanding this, commander Ramm did establish that he could pass through the Great Barrage and patrol the North Channel at the entrance to the Irish Sea without much difficulty. What's more, he would do so again, penetrating further into the Irish Sea and SQ-72 with devastating effect.

A report on Commander Ramm's first voyage by his superiors reads in part: 'First cruise of a new commander with a new boat. As a result of losing six crew to bring in three Danish steamers, sickness on board and numerous technical difficulties, very high demands were made on commander and crew, which the boat mastered. The captain encountered little traffic but used every possibility for attack, so the best can be expected in the future.'

Little did anyone know how prophetic these last few words would become.

UB-123: the final voyage

It had been six weeks since *UB-123* returned from her first voyage. The crew had been on leave with kin and loved ones before returning to duty at Wilmshaven. This proud harbour town lined with taverns and restaurants was thronged with jovial and celebrating sailors. Submariners were considered almost aristocratic, such was their pride and loyalty, but when they shared a meal or a beer across the table, they could not hide from one another the fear that the next voyage might be their last. The risks submariners took were such that they quite often did not suffer just damage from attack or near escapes - the event was often final and fatal.

It is difficult to understand how U-boat commanders at this point took on arduous and life-wasting, long distance raids such as Ramm's next one, when you consider the discontent in the forces at the time and the fact that an Armistice was being negotiated. But the loyalty of these commanders was considered to be of the highest and they continued their bitter attacks until the very day of surrender.

Up to 26 September 1918: When the crew had ended their celebrations, Ramm and his thirty-four comrades boarded *UB-123* and sailed for Heligoland sometime just prior to 26 September. As this was to be the submarine's final voyage, the log for this journey did not return to tell the tale. But the records and radio communications that were received from *UB-125* and *UB-123* were later edited by Admiral Arno Spindler and give some idea of the events during this voyage.

26 September 1918: Orders were received by Ramm and *UB-123* left Heligoland, sailing this time on a long voyage for the Irish Sea. Once again he sailed via the Kiel Canal and the Kattegat into the Skagerrak and through to the North Sea until he reached the western end of the Great Barrage. With more difficulty this time, he again eluded the dreadful mesh of mines and rounded the Orkneys through the Fair Isle Channel. The mine layers had been extremely busy in the area and the barrage was approaching completion.

1 October 1918: *UB-123* may have passed some time in the area of the North Channel but it was Ramm's intention to sail down the West coast of Ireland. Whilst in the North Atlantic, he may have contributed to the attack on the merchantman *Karmala* (8,983 tons) off the North West of Ireland. This vessel recorded an attack by torpedo which luckily missed.

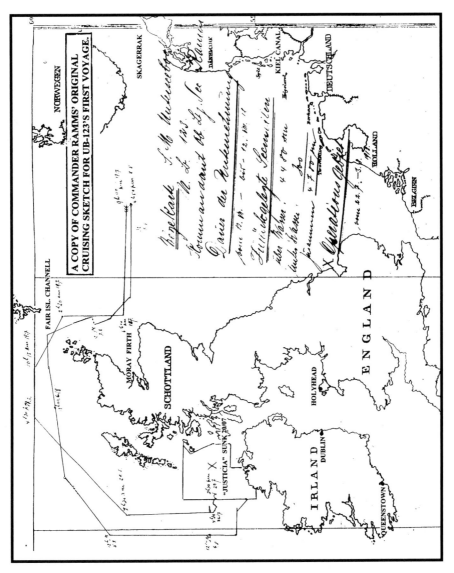

Official detailed sketch of UB-123's first long-distance raid

2 October 1918: Again in the North Atlantic, 40 miles North West of Tory Island, there was another attack which did not fail. This time it was the vessel *Arca* (4,837 tons) which was attacked without warning. The ship sank with the terrible loss of 52 sailors. This attack was in keeping with the time and place of Commander Ramm's journey to the South West of Ireland. (Unknown to Ramm and his crew, the U-boat base at Flanders was evacuated on this day.)

Every time a U-boat commander passed through the Fair Isle Channel to come 'North about', it was like cutting the umbilical cord with the Motherland. As the land mass of Scotland loomed up between the vessel and Scandinavian territory, it cut off the possibility of direct wireless communication. The only communication a U-boat could then make was with another U-boat and the Admiralty had ears.

Seven days passed in which there were no recorded attacks on shipping off the West or South coasts of Ireland. We can only assume that because of a lull during a change in U-boat patrols, the increasing effectiveness of Allied patrols and heavily escorted shipping in the South Western Approaches, that commander Ramm found difficulty in mounting any kind of an attack. In fact, at that time, there were so many warships available to the Allies, it had become almost suicidal to attempt penetration through the screens of destroyers escorting convoys in order to get a 'shot'. As well as all this, at that time U-boats had begun to concentrate their attacks in the areas of the North Channel, George's Channel and the Irish Sea.

10 October 1918: *UB-123* rounded the South West coast of Ireland. After taking land bearings, Ramm submerged and remained there until that night. Well after dark, he surfaced again to recharge his batteries and to give some time to his crew for fresh air and exercise. During the night a steamer passed close by without incident but Ramm was sure he had been spotted. After delaying longer than he should, daylight increased and he shouted down the pipe the order 'prepare to dive'. Just before he turned and entered the hatch to go below, he noticed the black funnel smoke on the horizon to the east. (The issue of the funnel smoke is a curious one in that none of the wartime depictions of the *Provinces* showed any funnel. Yet in the pre-war photos, funnel smoke was shown as 'black as night'. Was special smokeless fuel or a more advanced method of burning introduced to these mail steamers during the war years?) It was approximately 08.30 when he raised the periscope to take a look at the approaching steamer. The ship was approaching from his port beam at about 20 knots and he had a good idea as to the identity of the vessel. He knew from his earlier observations that he was situated in an area known to U-boats as Quadrant 524J but designated by the Admiralty as Square-72. This area of the Irish Sea included the track of the Holyhead-Kingstown mail boats.

After a few short minutes, his suspicions were confirmed when he identified the mail-boat *Ulster* steaming directly for him. The submarine was facing into a lumpy sea from the South with the light behind his oncoming target. He was ideally situated for an unsuspecting mail boat passing across his bows. When Ramm raised the periscope again he must have cursed with disappointment as the Ulster was then veering away at speed in a north-westerly direction. It was, of course, only following normal Admiralty instructions to steer a zig-zag course. The angle and distance had altered and Ramm knew he had lost 'the shot'. By the time the *Ulster* came about, it was

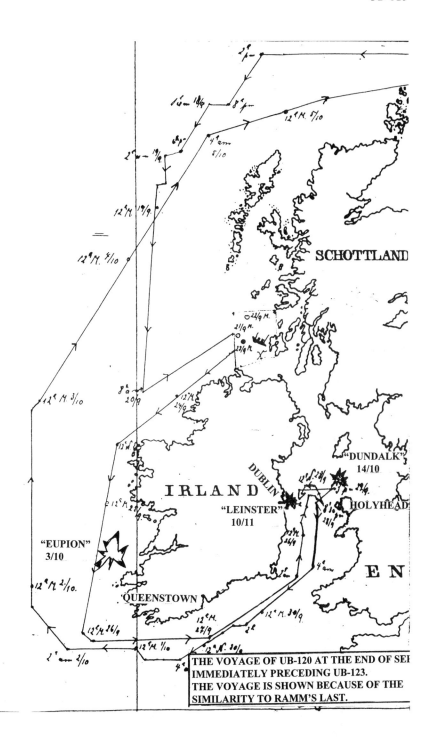

A recreation of UB-123's *last cruise from a similar one by* UB-120

drawing too close to the Kish Bank and it became increasingly more dangerous to risk positioning for an attack. He decided to neither alter nor jeopardise his position, but to wait. If he could remain undetected for long enough, he knew he had a good chance at a mail boat that almost certainly must return shortly. And it did.

The attack on the *Leinster*

The *Ulster* had come about and safely passed the *Kish Light Vessel* to the North. Coming out of the smoke from the disappearing *Ulster* was another packet travelling at approximately the same speed, but for some incredible reason not zigzagging. Commander Ramm could not believe his luck. In just a few moments, another equally valuable steamer was going to cross his bows. He did not know which mail boat it was - but it was the *Leinster*. Having none of the hesitancy reminiscent of his first cruise, he fired three torpedoes, the first of which missed. The following two struck their target and the *Leinster* exploded into a mass of debris and smoke, plunging to the bottom of the sea in minutes.

It was a 'text book' attack, technically brilliant and on a valuable target travelling at high speed. It was marred only by the loss of so many innocent civilians. To alleviate the suffering of those poor souls in the water, was it Ramm who sent the mysterious SOS? If it was a U-boat transmission, it would easily have been identified. German wireless had a distinct 'spark' in transmissions which the Allies were well acquainted with.

Despite a cloud hanging over the attack, the crew of *UB-123* considered the sinking of one of these cross channel mail steamers that had carried so many troops back and forth, and one which had escaped their comrades for so long, a great success.

Subsequent attacks

11 October 1918: The Swedish barque *Maja* (1,420 tons) was torpedoed and sunk off the coast of Co. Down. This attack is not attributed to Ramm and may have been the work of another submarine.

14 October 1918: Four more days of patrol in the Irish Sea passed before another suitable target presented itself. This time it was the turn of the small steamer SS *Dundalk* (794 tons) which was attacked five miles north west of Anglesey, North Wales. The *Dundalk* had left Liverpool during daylight 14 October, bound for her home port of *Dundalk*. Like the *Leinster*, the *Dundalk* was a twin screw steamer which was also considered a 'fast and safe steamer'. With the help of her deck gun she had successfully fought off a previous attack by a submarine. She had been built for the Dundalk and Newry Steamship Co. (DNSCo.) twenty-five years previously and had given excellent service.

The vessel was reported to have been 'torn asunder' that same evening by one torpedo, sinking her almost at once. Although damaged, two boats got away saving thirteen of the thirty-three people aboard. The two little lifeboats had quite an ordeal.

Having no food or water aboard, they were not picked up until after they were spotted by an aircraft the next evening. The sufferings of the survivors could have been made easier if the steamer *Carlingford* which passed close by soon afterwards had come to their rescue. Among the fatalities were the master, Captain O'Neill, and the general manager of the DNSCo., S.J. Cocks.

As the *Dundalk* was disappearing beneath the waves, the *UB-123* surfaced. The survivors reported they were only thirty yards off when they saw three crew on deck. Two of these manned the forward gun and one remained on the conning tower. This man was probably Robert Ramm. The survivors called out to the men on the deck but, not unusually, no recognition nor contact was made before the submarine disappeared again. (One of the crew of the *Dundalk* later testified that there was one gun forward and one aft of the conning tower. If this observation was accurate, it would put this submarine in the U class and rule out the claim that it was *UB-123* that sunk the *Dundalk*. This would ordinarily be correct if it were not for the fact that Commander Ramm definitely referred to a second deck gun.)

Situated at Portpatrick on the west coast of Scotland was one of many wireless listening stations which were scattered around the coasts of the British Isles. This station intercepted several German submarine transmissions between 10-13 October which could have come from submarines operating in the proximity of the Irish Sea at that time.

16 October 1918: *The SS Caloria* was torpedoed off Strathy Point, Northern Scotland. This is attributed to *UB-123* in Spindler's notes of 1940.

18 October 1918: Some eighty miles north west of the *Dundalk* incident, the merchantman *Hunsdon* (2,899 tons) met its end. It was torpedoed just off the entrance to Strangford Lough with the loss of one sailor. It is unlikely that Ramm made this attack and it is not known for definite to which submarine this attack is attributable. In any event, it would have been possible for Ramm to have returned via the west of Ireland but we are presuming that he made the attack on the *Dundalk*, in which case he may have taken the shorter but more dangerous route via the North Channel. This exit from the Irish Sea between the ports of Larne and Stranraer was extremely dangerous as it was an area which was intensely patrolled at that time, and even more so after an attack within the Irish Sea. The same applied also for the southern Rosslare-Pembroke exit. When Robert Ramm got out into the North Atlantic, he communicated by wireless with *UB-125*. This sub-marine had already been in the Irish Sea during September and had returned to Wilmshaven on 15 September. He had come out again and was just off Muckle Flugga in the Faroes when he made contact with *UB-123*. Robert Ramm obviously made known some of his exploits and inquired as to the most suitable position to cross through the Great Barrage again.

Whatever the details of the communication between the two submarines, Ramm again attempted to exploit the previous 'weakness' in the Western end of the barrage. Due to intensive mine laying while *UB-123* was on patrol, this area was no longer a 'weakness'. On 18 October, the Americans detected an explosion in the barrage at this end and presumed the incident to be due to the loss of *UB-123*. If the pressure hull had been ruptured, the submarine would have plummeted the eighty metres directly to the bottom with instant death for all inside. It may also have been only damaged superficially, in which case death would have come horribly slow. Either way, no trace was ever seen again of *UB-123*, thus ending the voyage and the lives of all of the young crew aboard. Neither the loss of all those who perished on the *Leinster*, nor of the patriotic crew aboard *UB-123*, had any influence on the outcome of the war, the end of which was so close to hand.

The above account of the last voyage of *UB-123* is based on the editing of submarine records by Arno Spindler in 1938-1941 and is generally accepted to reflect the ultimate fate of this submarine. Although I have added to it many of the sightings and attacks in the Irish Sea during that period, it is difficult, if not impossible, to corroborate the operations of *UB-123* which are based mainly on the presumption of its intended area of operations and its last radio transmission, the content of which was relayed by *UB-125* on 18 October. It is almost certain that at least one other submarine was operating in the Irish Sea at the time *UB-123* was present but which one it was remains uncertain.

A little more must be said about German submarine activity during the month of October 1918. Despite the presence of large numbers of US destroyers, submarine chasers, launches and even battleships out of Queenstown, and another large amount of similarly diverse vessels available to the British in the Irish Sea, a significant threat still remained here from submarines. Although German submarine radio transmissions were being successfully intercepted, U-boats still seemed to elude detection and enter this area with impunity. The only German submarine sunk in the Irish Sea for the entire period of the war was *U-87* off Carnarvon Bay in May 1918. Another six were sunk in its heavily patrolled approaches during 1918. The men and ships, and the new organisation that the Americans brought to the war had begun to tell.

Prior to 10 October, intelligence reports and the interception of German radio transmissions indicated that there was possibly more than one submarine en route to the Irish Sea. Confirmation of this suspicion was strengthened when two submarine sightings were made in the South Irish Sea on 9 October and one at the Kish in the early hours of 10 October (it is still possible that both these sightings were of the same submarine). At Holyhead, the Irish Sea Hunting Flotilla was deployed by flag captain Gordon Campbell VC from aboard the light cruiser *HMS Patrol* in various configurations off the coast of Anglesea and Rockabill, and south of the Isle of Man. The intention was to ultimately close in to detect these submarines and destroy them somewhere in the vicinity of Carnarvan Bay. This action was based on a weather report that the wind would veer east-south-east - this bay would give submarines a lee and an ideal striking position. Neither the wind nor the submarines proved to be predictable and, unfortunately for the *Leinster*, this left SQ-72 unguarded with disastrous results.

Not all German U-boat records were available after the war which causes difficulty in attributing specific attacks to a particular submarine. However, the vast majority of U-boat records were seized and copied by the Allies after the Second World War and these reveal enormous amounts of operational data. As they are extensive and held on microfilm in their original form in German, it takes a considerable amount of expense and time to extrapolate the relevant information. Nevertheless, the following preliminary data may help to throw light on the activities in the Irish Sea during October 1918.

There had been several attacks on vessels in September 1918 with eight ships sunk in the area of the Irish Sea during that month. With no respite, the month ended with the sinking of the *SS Baldersby* near the *Codling Light Vessel* on 28 September, heralding a relentless determination by U-boats for the coming October.

The following is a diary of submarine activity just prior to, and including, October 1918. Although incomplete, it serves to indicate just how much havoc and tension the U-boats brought to bear in the Irish Sea area so late in the war.

Submarine activity in the Irish Sea leading up to October 1918

29 August: *Guide Me II* sunk after collision off the Muglins.

29 August: *Atxeri Mendi* (2,424 tons) sunk by UB-125 off Wexford.

1 September: *Actor* (6,545 tons) struck by torpedo in the Irish Channel but reached port.

1 September: *City Of Glasgow* (6,545 tons) sunk by UB-125 off Wexford.

9 September: Commander Schrader of *UB-64* adds another victim to a long list and destroys *SS Barrister* (4,952 tons) south of the Isle of Man.

9 September: *SS Missanabie* (12,499 tons) sunk south of Cork by UB-87.

13 September: *M. J. Craig* (691 tons) torpedoed north-east of Black Head.

14 September: *Neotsfiel* (3, 821 tons) torpedoed south of *Skulmartin Light Vessel.*

15 September: *Energy* (89 tons) attacked and sunk by U-boat gunfire east of the *Codling Light Vessel.*

15 September: *Lackawanna* (4,125 tons) torpedo missed in the Irish Channel.

21 September: *Islandia* (2,069 tons) torpedo missed in the Irish Channel.

21 September: *Downshire* (368 tons) attacked and sunk by U-boat gunfire.

28 September: *Baldersby* (3,613 tons) torpedoed east of the *Codling Light Vessel.*

28 September: *Algores* (342 tons) torpedo missed in the Irish Channel.

29 September: Unknown (approx. 2,000 tons) Commander Plum of *UB-120* who spent several days operating in the Irish Sea at the end of September claims to have struck or sunk with a torpedo such a size of vessel on this date off the Kish.

29 September: *Nyanza* (4,053 tons) torpedoed 14 miles north-east of The Maidens.

30 September: *Sealark II* (182 tons) this hired trawler was sunk after collision of St John's Point.

30 September: *HMS Seagull* (735 tons) torpedo boats lost by collision in the Firth of Cylde.

4 October: The Japanese liner *Hirano Maru* is sunk in the George's or Bristol Channel area by UB-91.

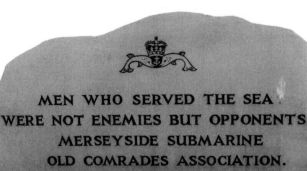

MEN WHO SERVED THE SEA
WERE NOT ENEMIES BUT OPPONENTS
MERSEYSIDE SUBMARINE
OLD COMRADES ASSOCIATION.
·1993·

OlzS	Robert	RAMM
LzS	Helmut	BAHR
LzS	Ferdinand	LOHMEYER
Strm	Johann	WYSCHKA
BtsMt	Richard	BERNSTEIN
BtsMt	Jac.	FRIEDRICH
BtsMt d.R.	Friedrich	HATTING
OMatr	Wilhelm	MOHRING
OMatr	Alfons	SCHWEBKE
Matr	Willy	FRICK
Matr	Jacob	JEUS
Matr	Emil	KRACKOW
Matr	Otto	OESER
Matr	W.	OSTERKAMP
Matr	A.	SCHERMER
Matr	Willi	SCHEEL
FkMt	Karl	KRAATZ
FkGast	Johann	ABENTHUN
Maschine :		
MarIng	Hermann	MEIER
Masch	Alfons	ELIES
OMaschMt	O.	FUHRMANN
MaschMt	Fritz	DROBBE
MaschMt		HUETTENRAUCH
MaschMt	P.	REINHARDT
MaschMt	August	REPP
MaschMt	Walter	SIEGLING
OMaschAnw	Richard	HOESTEREY
MaschAnw	Franz	BOEHLE
MaschAnw	Hermann	DONAT
MaschAnw	Erich	FUNKE
MaschAnw	J.	GERNANDT
Heizer	J.	BERNHOFER
Heizer	F.	ENGELMANN
Heizer	Emil	HUELS
Heizer	Adolf	LEVEREN
Heizer	Wilhelm	PLUECKER

Memorial stone at Cuxhaven and the 'missing' crew list of UB-123

It is clear that there were several submarines operating in the area of the Irish Sea around 10 October. This assumption is strongly supported by the fact that at this point in the War, U-boats were being advised to remain in contact with one another and to hunt in packs. Post-war speculation by Admiral Spindler has sug-gested that *U-90* may have been responsible for some of the attacks subsequent to that on the *Leinster*. Apart from sinking the American transport ship *President Lincoln* off the south-west coast of Ireland on 31 May 1918, I can find no other record of this submarine's activities. It may be that it has been confused with *UB-90* which was said to be out in this area but was lost in the Skagerrak on 16 October.

Other submarines with recorded operations in the Irish Sea during the closing stages of the war are *U-19, U-67, U-70, U-86, U-96, U-100, U-107, UB-62, UB-77, UB-89, UB-90, UB-91, UB-118, UB-120* and *UB-161*. There is a contemporary suggestion that *UB-121* was also in the Irish Sea and operating some sort of early inter-U-boat communication device with UB-123. The available U-boat records for *UB-121* end in September and for now this possibility will have to remain an aspect for further research. Without more detailed analysis, it is uncertain to say who was responsible for what.

Sightings of submarines and attacks by Allies in the Irish Sea in October 1918

9 October 1918: Submarine sighted off the Tuskar at 10.00.
9 October 1918: Submarine sighted off Bardsey, Wales at 11.40 (unlikely to be the same submarine as the first).
10 October 1918: Submarine sighted by *SS Sarah Brough* at 03.30 at the Kish.
11 October 1918: Submarine transmission intercepted from North Channel area. (The channel between Co. Antrim and Scotland - the North Channel - was sometimes called the Irish Channel.)
11 October 1918: Submarine (thought to be the *UB-123* attacked by seaplane out of Wexford.
13 October 1918: *HMS Lively* detected submarine north-west of the Isle of Man and attacked it.
16 October 1918: Submarine sighted 11 miles east of the Bailey.
18 October 1918: Submarine transmission intercepted from north-east of Ireland *(UB-123?)*.
18 October 1918: Submarine transmission intercepted claiming two attacks off Holyhead.
29 October 1918: *HMS Mallard* attacked target off the Skerries.

Shipping sunk in the region of the Irish Sea in October 1918

4 October 1918: *Hirano Maru* (7,936 tons) torpedoed in Bristol Channel (not in the Irish Sea but a very controversial sinking in an area which seems to be disputed).
6 October 1918: Ottranto (AMC 12,124 tons) lost in a collision off the Isle of Islay.
8 October 1918: SS *Neathead*. There is very little recorded or known about this vessel which may have been a converted steam trawler of 200-300 tons. Something

of a mystery still surrounds the circumstances of its loss several miles south of John's Point, Co. Down.

10 October 1918: *Leinster* (2,600) torpedoed east of *Kish Light Vessel*.

11 October 1918: *Maja* (1,420 tons) torpedoed off Co. Down.

14 October 1918: *Dundalk* (794 tons) torpedoed at Skerries, Anglesea.

18 October 1918: *Hunsdon* (2,899 tons) torpedoed off Strangford.

21 October 1918: *St Barchan* (362 tons) torpedoed off Co. Down.

29 October 1918: *HMS Ulysses* (1,090 tons) lost in a collision in the Firth of Clyde.

Unsuccessful attacks by U-boats

10 October 1918: *Sheerness* (1,274 tons) torpedo missed in the Irish Channel. This vessel had been attacked on three previous occasions, the most recent being in the Irish Sea on 22 August. This attack may also have been made by *UB-123*, as it occurred shortly after the sinking of the *Leinster*.

12 October 1918: *Laila* (1,626 tons) torpedo missed off north-east Ireland.

13 October 1918: *Darro* (11,484 tons) torpedo missed in Irish Channel.

18 October 1918: *Ulster* (2,600 tons) torpedo missed or failed to detonate in Irish Sea (unconfirmed).

22 October 1918: *Duke of Cumberland* (2,036 tons) torpedo missed in the Irish Channel.

22 October 1918: *Duke of Connaught* (1,564 tons) torpedo missed in the Irish Channel.

Chapter 5
Disaster in Square-72

First Officer Patrick Crangle

The following is a retrospective diary which covers the final hour of the Leinster and the following one hour and thirty eight minutes before the first survivor was plucked from the sea. It is based on the testimonies of Patrick Crangle - the ship's First Officer; Lieutenatnt H.L. Parker - the ship's adjutant; J.D. Mason - a chief mechanic with the USN; J.J. Higgins - the only surviving postal worker (out of twenty-two), and witnesses called to two subsequent inquests. It is also based on a report compiled by the Shipping Intelligence Office at Dublin and relevant and corroborating accounts from the censored daily newspapers in Dublin and Holyhead.

Absent from this account are the contents of a taped interview conducted with Mr William Sweeney at Roebuck Home, Dundrum, Dublin. Bill Sweeney was employed as Assistant Purser on the *Leinster* when she sank and survived to give a vivid re-collection of his experiences. The interview was given in 1979 and is quoted verbatim in chapter seven.

Diary of the final hour

08.00: It was the morning of 10 October and the mail packet steamer *Leinster* was making ready for her next cross channel journey from Kingstown to Holyhead. The mail train pulled into the sheds on the Carlisle Pier. The twenty-two postal sorters helped to heave the two hundred and fifty sacks of mail from the train and stowed them away in the deck below the forward hurricane deck (it was here that the mail was sorted during the crossing).

It was an overcast, hazy morning and almost eight hundred passengers and crew were boarding. The majority (in excess of four hundred) of those who boarded were soldiers. Left behind were many more who did not gain passage that morning. It was often the case that hundreds of soldiers and civilian passengers were 'shut out' and failed to get passage.

Whilst the majority of the crew were attending to boarding and baggage stowage, the principal officers met with Captain Birch on the bridge.

08.45: Following his customary daily consultation with the local Shipping Intelligence Officer, and before the sailing began, Captain Birch might have outlined the circumstances under which the crossing would be made. Although these were not totally unusual, they gave did give some cause for concern. Certain aspects of the journey needed to be made clear in order that everyone might be fully alert. The briefing was attended by First Officer Patrick Crangle, Second Officer Addison and Third Officer Mr Michlin. The ship's Adjutant, Lieutenant H.L. Parker, and chief wireless operator, A.J. Jeffries, would also have been present and the discussion may have proceeded along the these lines:

Firstly, let me tell you that we have a very distinguished American naval officer travelling with us today. He is Captain Cone of the US Navy who, you may remember, crossed a short time ago to visit bases in Ireland and is now on his return to headquarters in London. So, let us all be on our best behaviour once more.

Secondly, you are all probably well aware that the Navy has lost two of its patrolling drifters within the Bay during the past twelve months. The most recent was the Guide Me II in August, so I needn't tell you that patrols are a little stretched at the minute.

Thirdly, one of the scout airships was accidentally 'downed' yesterday at Malahide and will not be available to cover us. In any event, given the weather, it is unlikely that it would have of been of any assistance.

Lastly, and more to the point, you are all well aware of the numerous and increased submarine encounters these past few months and as recently as yesterday. You have also probably heard what might be exaggerated rumours of eight coal boats being sunk in the past week alone. (Freemans' Journal, 16 October).

You are acquainted with the problems the company has had in the past in their efforts to obtain escorts, and I regret to have to tell you that on this occasion we have again failed to obtain an escort. Despite pleading with the station commander, plus the fact that there are patrol boats alongside, I have been unable to persuade him to provide us with one. It would appear the protests by the crews earlier this week were to no avail. So, I am afraid we must once again depend on our speed and zig-zagging in order to avoid the possibility of an attack. Instruct the engineers to keep up a good head of

steam and make sure there are lookouts on the fo'c'sle. Inform the gunners
of our fears and tell them to keep a sharp look out.

Captain H.I. Cone

08.50: All of the mail sacks and the last of the passengers were now aboard. Fifty
prospective passengers were shut out.

The ship's adjutant settled all the military and informed them as to what part of
the ship they could or could not enter. (The rank of Ship's Adjutant was a little
unusual aboard a civilian vessel. It was a military rank but employed on a merchant
navy vessel. This was for the sole purpose of facilitating the management of the
large amounts of military personnel who travelled back and forth aboard the
Leinster. Lieutenant Parker had held the position since June following his recovery
from serious injures which he received while fighting in France. After fighting on
four fronts, Parker's appointment as Ship's Adjutant may have been seen as a
reward and considered a soft option in order to keep him out of harm's way, but as
we will see, he certainly brought a lot of enthusiasm to the job.)

08.53: The gangway was withdrawn from the port side of the *Leinster* and she
began her customary 180° manoeuvre. With the Carlisle Platform then astern, she
belched the familiar black smoke and steamed slowly past the lighthouses of
Kingstown's East and West piers for the last time.

09.37: After rounding the South Burford buoy, the *Leinster* steered north-east to
round the Kish Light Vessel. Having passed the lightship, the ship took on an
uncomfortable roll. The official description of the weather conditions was 'Wind
SSW 5 to 6 with a heavy sea running'. (For anyone unfamiliar with the Irish Sea,
any credible southerly wind will get up a very lumpy sea and, if travelling broadside
to it, can be extremely upsetting. There was a general perception that the weather was
not so bad at Kingstown that day, which is correct. But further out to sea the
conditions were a lot worse where the wind from that direction had more of an effect

on the sea state. The conditions were stated by some to be so bad that it forced several of the Admiralty's vessels back to port at Holyhead.)

The incoming *Ulster* was sighted and passed two miles to the north. The next and final leg of the *Leinster's* journey was reported to have been between eight to nine miles long, but the actual site of the shipwreck is just short of 5 miles east of the Kish lighthouse.

09.45: The *Ulster* was still visible on the horizon when more than one passenger shouted 'A torpedo'. This first torpedo was clearly described as having come from the port side and passed across the *Leinster's* bows. Although there were several lookouts on the fo'c'sle, it was never reported that they sighted it. Some passengers later stated that the vessel then veered to starboard, and this may be explained by the shipping intelligence report which stated that the 'master had just given the order to commence zig-zagging'. However timely or otherwise this instruction may have been, the ship was unable to avoid the next torpedo.

This second torpedo was seen by the lookouts who screamed the warning of its approach. A split second decision was required, and Captain Birch gave the order to 'put the helm hard a-port and starboard engine full speed astern'. This action, which was the standard procedure in such an event, would have had the following effects:

- The possibility of avoiding the torpedo.
- Giving the submarine a reduced target in the event of another shot.
- Putting distance between the ship and the submarine.
- More significantly, if sustained, bringing the ship full about 180° ready to return to the safety of Kingstown.

Before the manoeuvre could be completed, another torpedo came rushing at the port side where it struck the Leinster in the area of the busy sorting compartment. This was borne out by the almost total annihilation of this compartment, killing all but one of the twenty-two sorters. The sorting compartment of the *Leinster* was situated in what would normally be considered a 'secure' area, but this very quality meant that it became a tomb of steel for the postal workers. It was actually below the water line and accessed by two single flights of stairs, the second of which was the only access through the steel roof of the postal room. It was here that Mr Higgins worked, but at that time he was fortunate to be in an office compartment aft and partitioned from the remainder of the post room. It was this separation that saved Higgins from the full blast of the torpedo that came through the wall of the post room. What followed was clearly imprinted on his mind, and few have been so lucky to relate a similar tale: 'When the first torpedo hit the bow of the mail boat, it penetrated the port or left hand side of the bow, burst with a terrific noise inside, and blew a large portion out of the opposite side of the bow. This left two sides of the post office open to the sea and wrecked the interior.'

The compartment was plunged into darkness and the seawater rushed in from both sides of the wrecked hull. Mr Higgins called to his mates and with great effort struggled through the floating debris to where he expected the stairs to be. All he found was some light emanating from above, barely enough to locate an electrical cable hanging from the ceiling. Holding onto this he floated with the rising water and made good his escape through the opening at the top of where the stairs had been. This area was known as 'the shed' and for all but fellow worker John Ledwidge and one other, the rising water now sealed them from the remainder of their mates below.

His evidence continued: 'I put on my lifejacket [there were thirty situated in the postal room] and this was less than two minutes after the first torpedo had struck the mail boat. In that very short interval I saw the post office was completely filled with the inrush of seawater, and it was overflowing through the opening [the stairway] in the roof of the post office; ['the shed'] in fact, the seawater was about a foot deep on the roof.'

At this point Higgins was accompanied by John Ledwidge and soon after they met up with another postal worker, Pat Murphy. (There remains some confusion as to whether this was in fact Murphy or another postal worker, Tom Bolster.) Although Ledwidge made good his escape and reached a life raft, he died of exposure after about one hour. The other postal survivor, whom Higgins had believed to be Pat Murphy, had a broken leg but managed to get to the rails and lowered himself into the water. Unfortunately, he drifted in the wind and tide and was never seen again.

Mr Higgins concluded his graphic testimony: 'With the help of a rope I got to the lifeboat alongside, in which there were about 25 people, and almost immediately after, the lifeboat had to get clear of the mail boat which was sinking as a result of the second torpedo, which hit her in the centre and appeared to break her in two.'

You will recall that the *Provinces* were built of mild steel for speed, and in this area of the hull its thickness is described in the original specifications as being '15 lbs' (i.e.15 lbs per square foot.), tapering to '12 lbs at either end'. This is an equivalent thickness of 9.8mm. Giving nothing to over twenty years of service, this tenuous gauge of less than three-eighths of an inch may explain the awful damage the first torpedo caused to both sides of the vessel.

In more sympathetic circumstances, a U-boat commander may have left it at that after the first torpedo had struck, but bitterness and determination was driving these solitary U-boat skippers. On the one hand, a surrender was already being negotiated (orders were given only ten days later to cease attacks on such vessels). On the other, these skippers had travelled right around Ireland on many occasions in desperate attempts to 'get' one of these mail boats.

Although probably fatally damaged by the first torpedo, the *Leinster* turned sharply to starboard, diminishing its profile and opening the distance between it and the submarine. The boilers were soon 'blowing off' and, although the *Leinster* soon became pretty helpless, she continued on what was to become the disastrous course of coming right 'about' by 180°. Facing back towards Kingstown now, and robbed of her great speed, she began to settle by the head. The Leinster was helplessly positioned and presented a perfect 'starboard on' silhouette to the enemy submarine.

Commander Ramm of *UB-123* could not have had it easier. Unlike the circumstances of the attack on the *Lusitania* when Lieutenant Schwieger of *U-20* could not bring it on himself to fire another torpedo at 'this crowd of people struggling to save their lives', the third torpedo was loosed on the *Leinster*, totally annihilating it and causing the deaths of hundreds of people.

09.51: Whatever Commander Ramm's reasons - whether he felt the vessel was escaping, or didn't see the lifeboats being swung out (which might have been the case for the starboard side as the lifeboats were not swung out on departure as per instructions due to the bad weather), or he just simply wanted to finish the job - his third and final shot was conclusive.

This was, in fact, a dilemma for Ramm. If he departed the scene, he could not be sure of 'the kill' but if, on the other hand, he delayed to see the ship sink, he risked being discovered by the destroyers that would surely rush to the scene.

When the first torpedo struck, Officer Patrick Crangle rushed from his quarters where he had been making up the crew's wages. He ran for the upper forward boat deck and immediately began to prepare a lifeboat for launching. When he was there, he observed Second Officer Addison in conversation with Captain Birch and Captain Cone. Aft on the upper deck, Lieutenant Parker and USN Chief Mechanic Mason were also busy lowering lifeboats.

Clearly seen and recognised by Mason, the third torpedo left its wake of air-bubbles on its journey to the amidships on the starboard side. It struck in the area of the boiler room and although the boilers were already blowing off, it must have been their eruption that created an explosion that was described to be horrific and massive. Many on deck at the time were thrown into the air by the force of this explosion and all manner of metal and machinery rained down on those remaining on board.

10.01: Getting out the lifeboats had begun well but when the second explosion occurred and dispersed the officers, panic set in and resulted in several shameful incidents. But it had been a truly terrible explosion and those lucky to survive it must surely have been in a severe state of shock. The stern area of the ship seemed to fare best for the escaping survivors, with most having to jump from it. The ship sank quite quickly with its stern high out of the water and propellers still rotating.

(The depiction of the *Leinster* plunging vertically to the depths, bow first, is a customary image for ships 'going to the bottom'. However, in this case it is a little misleading. As the sea in this area is only 100 feet deep, when the ship reached such an angle there was less than a third of it down before it struck the bottom. The remainder of the ship would then just settle to the bottom.) *The Leinster* finally disappeared, entombing hundreds who hadn't had time to even come on deck. In the space of fifteen minutes, it was all over. From the moment the first torpedo struck to the minute the *Leinster* settled on the seabed, over five hundred people were dead or dying.

10.38: The Admiralty stated that its patrol boat (which had been alongside at the time of the *Leinster's* departure) reached the scene at 10.38, and when it arrived another destroyer was already there. This was a full hour and ten minutes - and in some cases, two hours - sooner than when many of the survivors stated they were picked up. A number and variety of vessels from all quarters arrived and effected the rescue of survivors from the freezing sea.

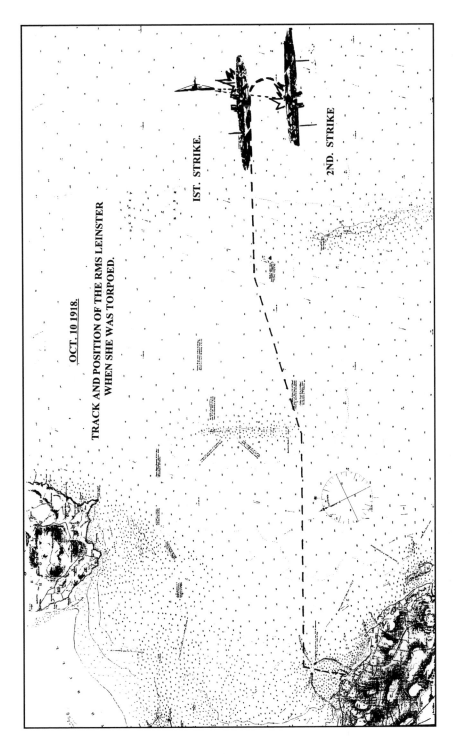

Track and position of the Leinster when she was toredoed

OCT. 10 1918.

TRACK AND POSITION OF THE RMS LEINSTER
WHEN SHE WAS TORPOED.

IST. STRIKE.

2ND. STRIKE

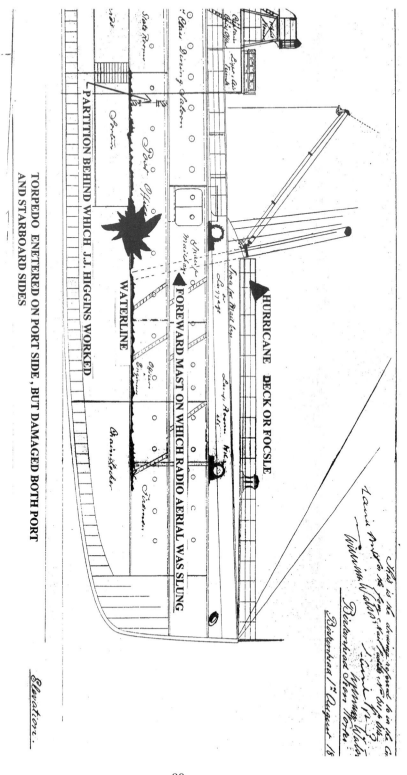

The second torpedo struck on the port side but the explosion penetrated the postroom to blow a hole in the opposite side of the hull

TORPEDO ENETERED ON PORT SIDE , BUT DAMAGED BOTH PORT
AND STARBOARD SIDES

PARTITION BEHIND WHICH J.J. HIGGINS WORKED

WATERLINE

FOREWARD MAST ON WHICH RADIO AERIAL WAS SLUNG

HURRICANE DECK OR FOCSLE

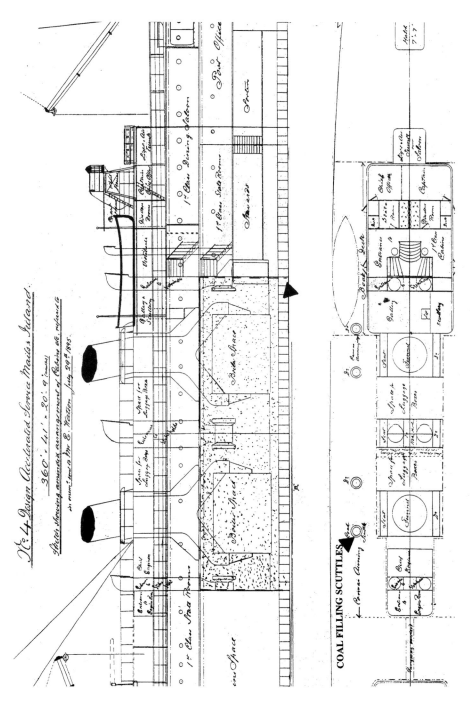

Position of the coal bunkers that existed on both port and starboard sides of the engine room - the approximate area where the third and final torpedo struck

The newspaper accounts were wide and varied - from heroism to cowardice, praise to criticism, great loss and fortunate rescue - and, despite the censor, many were accurate enough. Very few, if any, matched the wonderful report made by Lieutenant H.L. Parker, who seemed to have been a very gregarious type of character and was good with a pen. His report was made the next day, fresh and accurate in almost every respect (as far as I can determine from comparisons with other testimonies.) This report was never published. I have already, with others, used it in part to outline pertinent events of the sinking, but again, with its help, I will enlarge and fill in some of the more dramatic events and strange anomalies.

Although the *Ulster* had been delayed at Holyhead for fifty-five minutes 'waiting for an official starting time' from the Admiralty, there had been no indication or warning of any danger as the two mail boats passed near the *Kish Light Vessel*. For all anyone suspected, the journey was going to be quite regular, albeit a bit on the rough side. By then Lieutenant Parker had settled the troops. They filled the saloon making light of their return to duty. Upon leaving the saloon, he spotted the Chief Steward Lewis chatting with his brother who was a Shore steward. (There were three Lewis brothers and one cousin aboard.) Stopping for a chat, his account informs us: 'I had just left them when the ship was hit on the port side, forward, at about 9.37a.m. In compliance with my duties, I made for the bridge to report to the Captain. I reached the upper deck on the port side where I found one of the boats being lowered by several members of the crew.' (It was here he must have met chief mechanic Mason who was among those getting out of this boat.)

Parker went on: 'Two civilians (I believe one man was a priest) were getting into the boat, so I immediately caught the one who was partially in and threw him back and told him it was women and children first on this boat and if he tried to get in again I would kill him. Both apologetically explained that they were not trying to get into the boat. I am absolutely confident this statement was quite untrue. I stayed there for a few minutes until the boat was out of their reach, and lowered down, then rushed on to the bridge where I found Captain Birch standing talking to Captain Cone of the US navy.' (The very cool Officer Patrick Crangle, who had a long family tradition of seafaring, had already left this gathering to lower boats, and Second Officer Addison was also in this group.) Lieutenant Parker arrived at the bridge from where his story continues. 'I noticed the forecastle of the ship was well down but not completely submerged, and the ship maintained a perfectly even keel. I said to Captain Birch "I have come to report Sir, what are your orders." He replied, "Just wait a minute, Mr Parker." He then gave some orders to Captain Cone and turning to me said, "The wires are gone, so we have not been able to send a message. I am sure the ship will float".'

As an SOS was received, this statement by Parker had extremely tantalising ramifications. The anomaly it created did not escape the attentions of Admiral Bayly who later doggedly pursued this aspect of the affair. Could Captain Birch, who had had such long and varied experience at sea, have been mistaken? Radio experts say that if you are not transmitting successfully then it is immediately ap-parent. If Captain Birch was right, then who did send the SOS message? Does his use of the collective 'we' include Radio Officer Jeffries, Captain Cone, Second Officer Addison, or any of them? Captain Cone did survive the sinking and he confirmed in a six page report on 20 October that Captain Birch was doubtful on the issue of the emergency radio transmission. His words were: 'when I went to the bridge for the first time, he [Captain Birch] told me that he was very much distressed, but he was afraid that the wireless had not gotten through that we had been torpedoed, as the wireless was one of the first things damaged'. Is it possible that after Captain Birch left the radio room, the radio operator successfully transmitted, and if he did, did he fail or was he unable to inform Captain Birch?

Lieutenant Parker replied: '"I think it is extremely probable they will come back and hit us again Sir." He [Captain Birch] then put his hand in his pocket and withdrew a bunch of keys, selected one, told me to go down to the Chart Room, open the top drawer and bring him the weighted books. [These were the confidential operating instructions from the Admiralty which were weighted so that, when thrown into the sea, they would sink immediately to the bottom in the event of the ship been boarded.] I did as instructed and noticed his revolver, and going to the bridge again handed them over to Captain Birch. He then told me to go along to the boat deck and give orders for the rafts to be let loose. I did this and again returned to the bridge. I asked him if he had any further orders and he replied, "No Mr Parker, I have to thank you very much, you have done your duty, there is nothing more to do, it is now everyone for themselves."' Leaving the ship was far from the brave Captain's thoughts. Although these may have been the last words he spoke to Mr Parker, Captain Birch remained on the bridge with Captain Cone giving last minute instructions and assisting with the lowering of the boats until both of them were blown into the water from the force of the next explosion.

At this point we will discuss some conclusions from Mr Parker's detailed report:

• There was no SOS message sent! It is impossible to be absolutely certain on this point. As was stated, the Radio Officer Arthur Jeffries did remain in the radio room. But you will recall that the post room was devastated by the first explosion and the stairs blown away. These stairs were immediately ahead of the foremast (Signalmast) which passes from above through to the decks below, and on the top of which the telegraph wires were slung. Higgins also made no reference to a mast in the compartment to which he could have clung. Was it blown away or did the force of the explosion shake the aerial wires free by the force of the explosion? Yet a message *was* received.

• Despite the optimism from some of the passengers, Captain Birch knew the ship was going to sink one way or another.

• With some exceptions, the lifeboats *began* launching successfully.

Lieutenant Parker transcribed and signed his report the very next day when all of the previous day's events were fresh in his mind. He also knew at the time of writing that Captain Birch was not seen again after the second explosion. By way of respect to the Captain, Parker continues his report thus: 'I wish at this point to pay tribute to the perfectly cool manner in which Captain Birch conducted himself. He was absolutely calm and collected and a Britisher through and through in every sense of the term, reminding me, as he did, of the many stories I had previously read, of the traditions of the British Seaman. I feel proud to have sailed with him.'

THE SUBMARINE QUESTION : How it Stands.

Naval Vessels Rescuing Passengers from the Torpedoed "Leinster"

Drawn by D. Macpherson from eye-witness's description

Captain Birch had long understood the dangers on the cross channel route. He had expressed his fear of attack several times, most recently on the previous day on the bridge of the *Leinster* when he told a colleague that 'If this bridge goes under water, I go down with it'. He had also expressed fears that an attack from a lurking U-boat would come in rough weather. His words were indeed prophetic. In fact, he had been so convinced of the dangers that earlier that year he had refused to take a night sailing on an unlit sister vessel. (This arose when he was summoned at his home in Holyhead to attend company business - orders to sail were one thing, travelling in his own time was quite another.)

From the various accounts there is little doubt that Captain Birch behaved honourably and accomplished all, and more, of what was expected of him. For his trouble he was mentioned in the *London Gazette* for 17 January, 1919, where, along with many others, he received an expression of 'Commendation for his services from the King'. The King seemed to have valued the services of Captain Cone and the other brave officers in quite different ways, as we will discover.

To return to Lieutenant Parker's account of the sinking, the next episode in this horrible nightmare, which for many would quench the remaining spark of hope, was about to begin, but not before Lieutenant Parker exchanged his last few words with Captain Birch. 'Having completed my duties I saluted him, descended to the saloon deck on the port side, and requested all the passengers to keep perfectly calm and not to get excited. One lady who I am positive, was Lady Phyllis Hamilton, turned round smiling and said to me "We are quite all right, not a bit excited, don't worry about us". There was no panic or confusion whatever. I can truthfully say I did not see an excited person. The ladies were absolutely magnificent. I then proceeded down the saloon deck on the starboard side when the second torpedo hit her amidships.' (USN Chief Mechanic Mason was immediately above Parker on the upper deck and had seen the same approaching torpedo.)

You will remember from an earlier chapter that Lady Phyllis Hamilton was the lady who, when just a child, had accompanied her mother at the launch of the *Ulster*. An interesting and poignant supplement to the tragic loss of Lady Phyllis Hamilton was recently supplied by Edward Bayly who lives adjacent to Shelton Abbey in Co. Wicklow. Lady Phyllis Hamilton was visiting her sister Lady Wicklow here in 1918 and had a brief liaison with Edward's father, then an officer on leave from the British Army. In order to spend some extra time with him, she delayed her return to London by one week - until 10 October. Edward's father continued an illustrious military career in the Middle East and eventually married. He relates that his father seldom spoke of the tragedy but, following his death many years later, he found a locket of hair and a photograph of Phyllis Hamilton amongst his effects.

It is difficult to know if one could stay concerned for others, or even just composed, when scrambling for boats or rafts on a sinking ship or in a confused and cold rough sea. But however difficult it was, many managed to do this and were also very brave indeed. For some, this composure lasted for only a few moments longer. This moment was described later by both Mason and Parker, but for now, we will stick with Parker's account: 'Nothing more could be done as the whole interior of the boat seemed to be blown into the air. Many of the passengers were blown up with the explosion and many more were killed and injured by the falling debris. I was certainly of the last to leave the ship after she was hit a second time.'

Mason described in his report the final moments similarly: 'I saw the second torpedo coming directly for the starboard side. This torpedo hit about amidships, in the vicinity of the boilers, which apparently exploded, even though I noticed that the boilers were being blown through the safety valves from the time the first torpedo hit. The second torpedo and boiler explosion produced an enormous amount of wreckage which fell so thickly in clouds together with steam and debris, that it was difficult to see anything at all. It was impossible to control the people after the second torpedo hit and there was a rush for the boats and rafts. The ship listed to port and went down by the bow. I left the upper deck and lowered myself over the stern with a rope.'

This second strike amidships on the starboard side was in a critical area - the very heart of the ship. Here the four boilers were situated and, although said to be already 'blowing off', would have been at full working pressure. These were surrounded on two sides by coal bunkers. Outside that again, and rising in the forehead compartments, was the inrushing seawater. This whole engine room area, however slowly, was being pressurised by the rising water and was priming for an awful explosion. The explosion was described by almost all the survivors in similarly graphic details, the principal aspect of which was their surprise at the violence and devastation that it caused. It has more recently been suggested by experts that the second massive explosion in the *Lusitania* was caused by the combustion of the coal dust in empty bunkers. We do not need to look for the cause of the second explosion in the *Leinster* as it was due to the second torpedo. But an explanation of the ferocity of its effect may be open to some dispute and I should not leave out the following facts just because they are uncannily similar to those on the *Lusitania*.

When the *Provinces* were built, they were specified to have 'about 100 tons coal capacity'. Quite rarely the maximum they ever took was 110 tons. Bunkering was carried out every day at Holyhead only and the round trip consumed between 41 and 50 tons. The meticulous coaling records kept by the CDSPCo clearly show that the last bunkering of the *Leinster* took place at Holyhead on 8 October (48 tons). Although a round trip was made on 9 October, there is no bunkering record for that day. Theoretically, two round trips could be made without refuelling, but with precious little exception, this was seldom ever attempted. If this record is not a clerical error, it means that the Leinster made her last journey on 10 October with very little coal in her bunkers. The obvious and similar conclusions to those drawn in the case of the *Lusitania* can again be hypothesised in this case. These were that the first explosion rocked the vessel and erupted the bituminous dust within the coaling bunkers. The ship then began to sink and compressed dust filled air spaces within the engine room. Primed, this inflammable combustion was then ignited by the explosion from the second torpedo. With the resistance of the water around the boilers being greater than the decks above it, due to the large areas cut away for ventilation, the explosion erupted through the upper deck with dramatic and devastating effects.

All of those on the upper deck in the vicinity of the bridge seemed to have been blown from it into the water. First Officer Crangle was one of these and he received serious head injures during the fall. His watch stopped in the water at 09.55. Patrick Crangle's broken watch and the time it showed became a point of reference for the inquest, and much of the subsequent timing of events, torpedo strikes, radio messages, rescues, etc. related to it.

Many survivors, such as Mason, clambered over the stern of the sinking *Leinster* before she slipped under the water. Lieutenant Parker was also among them. He described his escape and its harrowing aftermath in his report: 'I climbed down a trailing rope into a boat which had been lowered but there was some difficulty in getting free, as the lowering ropes, fore and aft, were still attached to the ship. I handed my pocket knife to a sailor who was standing in the bow of the boat and he succeeded in cutting the ropes there. The stern ropes were ultimately got clear and the boat got away just before the ship sank. The boat into which I had dropped was well crowded so I dived overboard and swam to a raft about 20 yards off. On arriving there I looked round and saw the stern of the *Leinster* high in the air and at that moment realised some person was clinging to my leg.'

Lieutenant Parker's brave exploits were not finished. Surprised by the clutching at his leg, he continues his tale: 'I found this to be a lady and I pulled her alongside on to the raft. On looking round again the ship had disappeared. A few seconds later the lady whom I got hold of recognised her husband clinging to an upturned boat; simultaneously he recognised his wife. He shouted to me "For God's sake look after my wife", and I promised to do so as long as I survived. I had the good luck to support her until we were ultimately rescued.' (The lady in question was wife to Second Lieutenant Marsham Rae of the 2nd Yorks Dragoons who was not so fortunate and drowned.)

Lieutenant Parker estimated that his experiences in the water lasted two hours before the British destroyer *HMS Mallard* arrived at the scene. He described the last desperate moments thus: 'On the raft with me were two soldiers and a lady. The sea was very rough indeed and a moderate gale was blowing. At times the wind seemed to increase and seas broke over us several times. We suffered severely from the cold and stiffness, and one of the soldiers hanging on to the raft evidently went mad; he let go, slipped off and was drowned. Another soldier had a similar experience and tried to climb onto the raft. I ordered him not to do so as it was positively going to mean the loss of us all, but he clung onto the lady and refused to let go. I ordered him to let go and work round to a better position on the raft, but he cursed me and kept dragging the lady down. All the time he seemed to be quite mad, so realising the danger to the others, I forced him to relax his grip and pushed him off with my feet. I threw him a grating and another lifebelt but he sank.'

In his own words, Parker recalls that, with difficulty, his raft companions were hoisted aboard the *HMS Mallard* where they were cared for with great kindness. He also reflected on the scene that he had left behind. 'I saw four boats [there were ten lifeboats aboard the *Leinster*] that had got safely away from the ship filled with passengers, nearly all civilians, although one was upset by a big sea a few minutes later. A number succeeded in climbing on to the upturned keel but the majority were swept away and drowned. I saw many dead and drowning with lifebelts on and properly adjusted, and this was undoubtedly due to the heavy seas breaking over the survivors. Had the sea been calm, many more would have been saved. In my opinion the rafts were safer and did greater service than the boats. We reached Kingstown about 3pm and the survivors were taken to the various hospitals and hotels.'

Parker's report is extremely revealing and gives much upon which to ponder. It is unfortunate that it was not explored by inquiry or inquest, nor indeed was Chief Mechanic Mason's. His report was also made to his superior officers and not released. His experience was not all too dissimilar to that of Parker's and we will take it up as he enters the water. 'I swam to a hatch and then to a raft. I looked back and saw the ship sink. At the time there were not more than four or five lifeboats right side up in the water and I believe all of them must have been capsized. There were at least a dozen rafts which floated clear but it was very rough and very difficult to stay on the rafts or to hold onto them when they became crowded. I tried three different rafts, staying on the last one until taken off by *Motor Launch 154*. As I went to the third, Captain Cone was holding on and in reply to my question as to how he was doing, he told me both his legs were broken. The Captain, two US Naval enlisted men (I think Aviation Quartermasters), one civilian and myself were the only ones holding onto this raft. The raft capsized twice and the sea so high that we could do nothing but hold on to it and pieces of passing wreckage in an effort to hold the raft steady.

'I was in the water holding on to this raft about an hour and I would estimate that we were not picked up until two hours from the time the ship was torpedoed. There was considerable difficulty in getting the Captain aboard the motor launch, each of us in turn trying to hoist him up. Finally, one of the crew jumped overboard and made a line fast to him and he was hoisted aboard. The Captain, officers and crew of the *ML 154* treated us with great consideration and did everything possible for us which could be done. This little boat with only half the crew on board, picked up altogether twelve or fourteen and by promptly leaving the scene when no more people who were alive and could be found, undoubtedly saved those that they had rescued, who were the most seriously injured and exhausted. The crew of this boat deserve great credit for gallant and untiring action and for the apparently excellent condition of their machinery when run at utmost speed. Fortunately the *ML154* had some whiskey aboard which, in the absence of medical attendance, under the conditions was very much appreciated. Captain Cone was so exhausted that he could not drink but when his lips where moistened with a little whiskey, his condition was perceptibly improved.' (This practice is utterly frowned on today!)

Following some further reporting, Mason went on to praise a local officer from Kingstown. 'Lieutenant E. Unwin of the *ML 154*, who was at the wheel and to my mind handled the little boat excellently, took me up to his house after landing at Kingstown and was extremely generous and considerate in his treatment. The entire part taken by *ML 154* during this accident cannot be too highly praised.'

HMS Lively was first to reach the scene followed closely by *HMS Seal*, both of which suffered some damage at expense of the rough passage. After receiving the relayed SOS, *HMS Mallard* also dashed to the scene at top speed and in so doing swept away its bridge in heavy seas. When she arrived, Captain Boyd attended to one of the *Leinster's* lifeboats. This was the No. 5, from the port side. He was unable to hide his disgust at finding only five persons in it who were crewmen from the *Leinster*. After inquiring from them had they not been able to aid any of the survivors in the water, he ordered them into the destroyer and replaced them with some of his own crew. They made several journeys back and forth plucking survivors from the water and rafts.

Second Officer Addison and Captain Birch had been blown up with the second explosion. Addison was killed outright but the Captain was thrown into the water. Sometime later a lifeboat, with the frequent mail boat passenger and travelling salesman Mr Hood in it, recognised the floating Captain Birch and came to his aid. The Captain's head was badly injured and he had at least one smashed leg. They tried in vain to haul him into the boat, but it was as much as they could do just to keep his hands on the gunwales. The occupants of this lifeboat were also rescued by the *Mallard*, but when they came alongside, a somewhat regrettable incident took place. The lifeboat had been taking in water and when a chance of survival presented itself there was a rush to the safety of the destroyer. With the weight within the boat taking a sudden shift, the boat capsized. Captain Birch lost his grip and disappeared under the water and was not recovered for some days. This upset Mr Hood so much that he later regretted that the Captain had not been got aboard first. (It was also regretted subsequently by several others who had been in the lifeboat and reached safety. The Captain was a man who had stayed with the ship to supervise the lowering of the lifeboats until he was blown off it.)

Captain W. Birch

In another of the lifeboats, a second pitiful scene was taking place. In this boat was the chief steward Mr Lewis who had been chatting unsuspectingly with his brother and Parker just prior to the first explosion. It was Mr Lewis and the MP Alderman Joyce who had helped lower this boat and, with great pains, succeed in getting some of the ladies and a one-legged officer aboard. They subsequently spent an arduous two hours in the lifeboat having to continually bail out the boat as the

99

rough sea came over the side. They steadied the boat with a sea anchor and proceeded to pick up some more survivors from the water. Sadly the brave Lewis lost his two brothers and a cousin when the ship went down.

From both Dublin and Kingstown many craft of different types eventually reached the scene rendering assistance to various degrees in very rough seas. The Admiralty records of the disposition of the Irish Sea Flotilla at the time are provided on the next page. From the chart and the report by Commander Dennison, it is difficult to understand how *HMS Lively*, which was furthest from the scene by at least eight miles, could have overtaken all other vessels to reach the scene first.

Although sometime later, the drifter Formidable also attended but in her case it was to drop depth charges on an oily patch, which turned out to be the resting Leinster. It was as if to finally seal the fate and create a legend of the doomed mail boat. The following day the newly delivered seaplanes at Wexford recorded their first attack on a submarine which was said to be the one that sunk the *Leinster*. The bombs are meant to have dropped near to the submarine which immediately dived and emitted oil in the area for some days later.

Of the officers who were on the bridge of the *Leinster* that fateful morning, Captain Birch was killed and was commended as already described. Addison and Jeffries were also killed but I can find no mention of commendation for either of these. First Officer Patrick Crangle received injuries to his head and legs from which, his family stated, he had never really recovered when he died five years later. And although he gave his place in a lifeboat, choosing to trade places with a lady in the water, I could find no commendation for him either.

As we know, Lieutenant Parker survived and reached the safety of Kingstown. As he strolled from the Victoria Wharf in pyjamas and dressing gown, he was cheered by the large crowd which had gathered. It was not because they had learned of his heroic conduct, but more for the casual stride with which he emerged from the scene. As he said himself: 'I felt none the worse for my experience and proceeded to a hotel.' Had the crowd been aware of the earlier events and the part he played in them, I suspect he might have been carried to the hotel. Although on the outside he may have seemed nonchalant, on the inside he might have agreed with his namesake M. Parker who wrote:

> *Ye gentlemen of England*
> *That live at home at ease,*
> *Ah! little do you think upon*
> *The dangers of the seas.*

For Lieutenant Parker also, I have been unable to find a commendation but according to Bill Sweeney he was awarded a 'life saving medal'. Practically all of the principal naval personnel were nominated for some kind of commendation or other. Captain Cone was recommended by Admiral Bayly and commended on the incident thus: 'A Letter of Commendation from Admiral S. Sims' and 'Honorary Commander of the Military Division of The Order of the British Empire in recognition of his gallantry in saving lives on the occasion of the torpedoing of

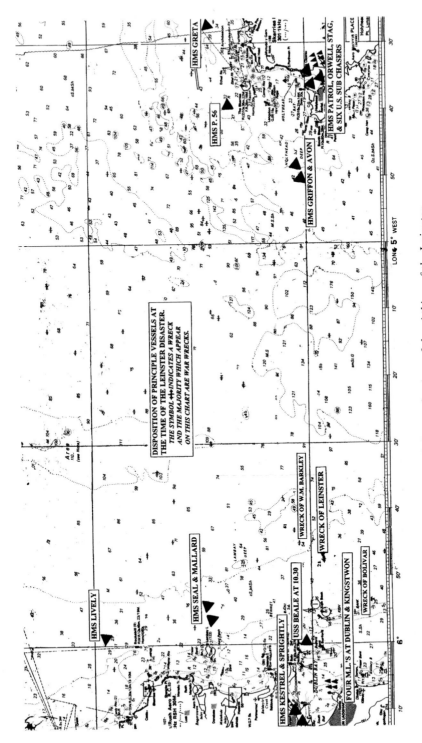

The disposition of the Admiralty vessels in the Irish Sea at the time of the sinking of the Leinster

HMS *Leinster.*' Not to detract one bit from Captain Cone's brave contribution and the extensive injuries which eventually contributed to his early placement on the Retired List in 1922, I sincerely hope that this 'singling out' was not remorse for having British patrol boats idle alongside at Kingstown and US ones at Holyhead while important American Allies were being attacked, at least one of which later rushed to the scene with a speed which the Admiralty was unaware it possessed.

As Captain Gordon Campbell put it, it was important '... to inspire confidence and save panic ...' so the *Ulster* sailed again that evening with the mail and was escorted by *HMS P56*.

Chapter 6
What the papers said - and what they didn't say

There is little doubt that the quality of wartime reporting has altered dramatically since that which took place during the First World War. Firstly, the number of media through which the reports can be transmitted are infinitely more varied. Secondly, the consumer's appetite for quality and accurate reporting is continually being heightened. Wherever possible, the reporting of battle situations, such as the Falklands and Gulf Wars, were and are still managed and censored for media consumption. But, generally speaking, we enjoy the potential for far more freedom and accuracy in wartime reporting. For example, a brave journalist or cameraman has only to inveigle his way into a situation with a mobile phone and hey presto, the report or pictures are on the news desk anywhere in the world. Up-to-the-minute digital apparatus contained in a small briefcase can transmit pictures around the world and, as we recently witnessed in Eastern Europe, news can be broadcast over the Internet. But the last word still remains with the news media's producer or editor - or is it with their owners?

During the First World War, sinkings or attacks on Allied shipping were either not reported at all or, at best, belatedly reported in brief. The reason, of course, was censorship in order to deprive the enemy of valuable information. It was only when something was unavoidably detected by the public that restricted reporting was allowed. Occasionally there were 'other' reasons for allowing regulated reporting of a war incident - in other words, when the news was 'managed'. This can only happen when the State has the power to control the press completely. It then becomes a powerful manipulative tool, and its original aim of depriving the enemy of intelligence can become a convenient mask for mischievous propaganda. The extent of censorship in 1918 is quite difficult to comprehend. It was not just an extension of what it is now, i.e., obtaining court orders to prevent articles and books (although often only temporarily) from going 'into print'. It controlled all aspects of reporting with an iron fist, including the comings and goings of reporters and the distribution by news agencies of all printed material. It controlled the printing of all articles, including *Letters to the Editor,* an issue that affected the production of the *Dublin Evening Telegraph* in October when the paper printed a letter received from a reader criticising the arrest and imprisonment of a citizen. In 'Defence of the Realm', the paper was halted until the proper undertakings were given by the editor. It must also be stated that it is convincingly argued that censorship during war is very necessary, and that owners and editors of newspapers played, and do play, a willing part.

As far as Ireland was concerned, during October 1918, there were two aspects that were of particular interest to the British authorities. One was the growing aspiration of its population for 'Home Rule', and the other was a stream of accusations on the lack of enthusiastic 'volunteers' for the 'Great War' which might necessitate the introduction of 'Conscription'. A troublesome Irish thorn in the British side was the constant political unrest. It was more than just inconvenient to have the subjects of your most strategically positioned Colony constantly in a state of agitation during such a critical period. The rebels were relaying infor-mation of British activities and were developing links with the German government in the hope of receiving aid for an armed insurrection - attempts which we know were unsuccessful more than once. This was in contrast to another section of the population which worked all the hours God sent producing munitions and repairing and constructing the British war machine and, of course, volunteering to lay down their lives defending the Realm. Most of this loyal fervour has been attributed to the economic state of the country at the time and the relatively poor conditions of the working class. It is often forgotten that in Ireland, Germany was generally seen as the aggressor and there did exist a great deal of patriotism and loyalty to the Crown.

Conscription, or the lack of it, was always a tricky issue and became one of special interest not only to Britain but also to the USA. In 1918, the American Press printed the view that 'the enemies of conscription were no friends of the Allies'. This misguided comment was made despite the fact that thousands of Irish vol-unteers had already lost their lives or suffered terrible wounds in the foul, infected trenches throughout Europe. Amongst the afflictions these volunteers had to endure was the horrible effects of gas poisoning which they suffered from for the remainder of their 'pension'. The figures show that despite the rantings of touring recruiting officers, it was very difficult to get the numbers up during the latter stages of the war, especially in places like Limerick and Sligo.

Although between June and October of 1918, ten thousand more Irish volunteers had enlisted in 'defence of the realm', it nevertheless did not prevent the normally eloquent speeches made by some of the visiting recruiting officers being exasp-eratingly reduced to threats. They warned the listeners that if the numbers were not forthcoming, conscription might be introduced which would 'double' the existing number of voluntary recruits from each County. On the other hand, it is popularly argued that, as Britain was fighting a difficult war with a powerful enemy, the last place they wanted nests of malcontent and armed Sinn Féin sympathisers was 'in the ranks' - although God knows they could do little damage with the sea behind them and the Hun in front. The plain truth was that the threat of conscription was of more value than all the rebellious conscripts that could be rounded up under the actual policy of conscription itself. Newspapers on 15 October gave the Irish recruiting returns. The figures in brackets show the number required from each area by 15 October - the same day.

The difficulties with the flagging volunteer returns was about to get a shot in the arm, courtesy of the German navy and the British censor. The *'Leinster Outrage'* provided the catalyst for a media onslaught against the 'German Hun' with outpourings summoning every decent citizen in a call to 'do his duty'. It was only if you noticed the insertion 'As passed by the censor' that you could even suspect that maybe all was not as it appeared in print. In the Chief Censor's own words in 1920, such an insertion 'was never a guarantee of truth but in the censor's judgement the statement would not be of benefit to our enemies, or harmful to the interests of this country'. It is true there are those whom you cannot fool, but considering the altogether total grip the establishment had on the media, it must have moulded the opinions of a sizeable majority of the population.

Irish recruiting figures	
Dublin..........2,291 (11,700)	Omagh..........845 (5,700)
Belfast..........3,576 (8,500)	Galway.........196 (2,900)
Cork...............689 (4,700)	Armagh.........313 (2,400)
Limerick.........528 (5,200)	Mullingar......316 (1,800)
Waterford........708 (5,200)	Sligo.............167 (1,600)
Total for all Ireland.............9,629 (50,000)	

First reports of the attack on the Leinster appeared in several newspapers on the following day, the most dramatic and comprehensive being in the 'Special Edition' of *The Freeman's Journal* on 11 October. However, a 'Stop Press' edition of *The Evening Herald* on the actual evening of the sinking - Thursday 10 October, 1918 - was seized and withdrawn, allowing only the normal and earlier issue to be circulated without any mention of the sinking of the Leinster. *The Evening Herald* was shut down that same evening and was not allowed to publish again. In fact the special powers emanating from Defence of the Realm Act not only shut the Herald's premises in Abbey Street, but the 'G' men from Dublin Castle, under Inspector Mulvehill, also descended on the works to dismantle and remove the paper's presses and machinery. (This was no idle threat as *The Kilkenny People* had discovered to its surprise and expense a year earlier.)

What, then, did the offending report say? *The Irish Independent* was not affected and it printed with 'permission', in its Saturday edition, the reason for the withdrawal of the 'Stop Press' issue of *The Evening Herald*. (Some printing of this issue may have taken place but no copies are available.) Contained in the 'Stop Press' edition were the two offending sentences which had been run as an 'official' statement received from the Press Bureau in London. (The Press Bureau was the official office where the various Ministries disseminated their releases for publication.) The *Herald's* editor therefore did not think that he needed to get the article approved by the censor in Dublin. This would seem to be reasonable enough, and the two sentences in question were printed reading as follows: 'The City of Dublin steam mail boat was torpedoed and sunk this afternoon in the Irish Sea. It is understood she carried a full compliment which are all believed to be safe.'

It is difficult to understand why two obviously incorrect sentences should necessitate the closure of the paper. There is much you can read into it but given the insufficient information available, the only reason I can see is the obvious but inadequate one. That is, if the report had been received from the official mouthpiece of the Crown and printed, in good faith, subsequent revelations to the contrary might have lead to embarrassing questions.

- If the release was made to the *Herald,* for what reasons was this incorrect statement made? It might seem that it was the intention of those in authority to control and drip feed the awful casualty figures as it saw fit.

THE GREAT WORLD WAR : WEEK BY WEEK.

On Saturday of last week (October 12) Germany carried her peace negotiations a step further by accepting the famous fourteen points laid down by President Wilson on January 8 last as conditions precedent to the conclusion of peace; moreover, the enemy also accepted the additional four points set forward by the President on February 11. As a preliminary to the discussion of peace terms by a "Mixed Commission," Germany proposed to evacuate the invaded territories of France and Belgium. Seeing that the evacuation of the territories in question is in any case only a matter of time, the German offer is cunning rather than generous; certainly for Germany an evacuation arranged by armistice is greatly to be preferred to one arranged by Marshal Foch. She, no doubt, hoped by this means to withdraw her armies unbroken from the field and to salve her guns and material of war, and incidentally to be able to boast to future generations that she had faced almost the whole world in war—and had not been beaten in the field. Presumably, too, she intended to be represented on the "Mixed Commission" appointed to settle the peace terms; "expiation" is not yet in her war vocabulary, and Germany has not yet realised that she is an outcast among the nations, the "untouchable" among the castes of humanity.

Moreover, while the enemy tendered this imitation olive branch to the Allies, German submarines were pursuing their trade of murder on the high seas, and the Irish mail boat, *Leinster*, was sent to the bottom with a loss of nearly six hundred souls, chiefly women and children, and northern France was being laid waste with systematic rapacity and thoroughness. Neither must it be forgotten that it is the chief wealth-producing and industrial districts of France which are being thus destroyed and stripped of their machinery.

Lafayette

Lady Alexandra Phyllis Hamilton

One of the missing from the S.S. "Leinster." She was a daughter of the Dowager Duchess of Abercorn and a sister of Lady Wicklow

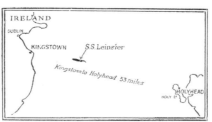

The Torpedoing of the Irish Mail Boat, "Leinster"

This map shows the approximate position of the "Leinster" in relation to Kingstown and Holyhead. The "Leinster" was hardly out of sight of land when she was struck by a torpedo on October 10 and sunk, with a loss of over five hundred lives

Germany's present attitude renders acceptance of her offer impossible; that an unconditional surrender in the field could be the only basis of a profitable discussion was the opinion expressed everywhere in this country and America. The Allies' opinion is aptly summed up by *The New York Tribune*, which says: "We wish the President had said to Prince Maximilian: 'The conditions you refer to are for discussion between the American Government and its Allies. They will represent our agreement on the state of the world henceforth. It is not for you either to decline or accept those conditions. We will impose them upon you. The only thing we will accept from you is unconditional surrender.'"

There is one point in those set forward by President Wilson which particularly concerns this country, namely, that which deals with the "absolute freedom of navigation upon the seas." "This," says a correspondent writing to *The Morning Post*, "would not exclude Count Reventlow's interpretation of the phrase in his Berlin speech of March, 1917, when he declared that freedom of the seas meant for Germany the possession of 'such maritime territories and such naval bases' as 'to guarantee ourselves the command of the seas . . . we want such a jumping-off place as would give us a fair chance of dominating the seas.' That means the filching of the Trident. For these islands it is vital that we should maintain unimpaired all these maritime rights sanctioned by the Law of Nations."

On Tuesday President Wilson's reply to Germany's proposals was made known. There can be no parley with Germany while she continues her cruel and inhuman practices on sea or land. The question of an armistice can be settled by the commanders in the field alone; there can be no dealings with Germany's present rulers.

Copyrighted in the U.S.A.   *Drawn by R. M. Paxton*

While Germany Spoke of Peace—The Sinking of the S.S. "Leinster" in the Irish Channel

The Irish mail boat, "Leinster," was torpedoed on Thursday of last week when outward bound from Kingstown. Two torpedoes were fired, the second striking the vessel in the engine-rooms and causing her to sink in a few minutes. There was a considerable swell at the time, which made the work of launching the boats exceedingly difficult, and many people were killed by the explosion caused by the second torpedo. Terrible scenes were witnessed during the time which elapsed between the sinking of the vessel and the arrival of the rescuing destroyers, most of the victims being women and children

- If this statement was not released by the Press Bureau, would the *Evening Herald* concoct such an obvious mistruth and risk the wrath of the censor? This seems very unlikely and if you accept this to be the case why then would those in authority change their mind and allow almost full reporting of the disaster?

Whatever the reasons, it would seem that the *Evening Herald* would have to be closed if only to give weight to the statement of the erroneous nature of their journalism. Even so, it still seems the closure was rash and an inappropriate reaction. Who knows what was true or not when such restraint was wielded over the Press? The answer to this may lay in the subsequent board room minutes of that paper. These, I was informed, were unavailable for viewing.

The situation was saved after the paper's owners' offered to commence a distress fund with 150 guineas for the victims of the *Leinster* and the appropriate compliance and undertakings were given. Nevertheless, production of the paper was not allowed for four more days until the following Tuesday.

Reports on the tragedy, were, as you might expect, very similar to those on the sinking of the *Lusitania*. In fact, one article was headed *'Ireland's Lusitania'*. (There seems to have been some confusion about whether the *Lusitania* was a British or an American tragedy.) A brief but absurd knee jerk reaction by the authorities to belay fears was the circulation of a rumour that the *'Leinster* was being towed back'. This failed miserably. How, or more to the point, why this remark was made is a mystery, as the *Leinster* had already sunk before its publication. Initially unaware of the scale and the full extent of the disaster, but later faced with the prospect of bodies being washed ashore and recovered by all manner of vessels, there was nothing for it but to allow what might have appeared to be full reporting on what everyone could see with their own eyes. But a 'damage limitation' exercise got into gear too.

There were many first hand accounts of the loss of kin and friends, startling and emotional rescues, ironies and coincidental grief and so on. It is impossible to reprint all of these but the following two appeared in *The Freeman's Journal* and were typical of many others:

A BRIDE OF YESTERDAY

The bride of a Canadian named Frizalle (who married the previous day), was lost under very tragic circumstances. They were to return to Teignmouth, but when they arrived at the Mail Boat, Frizalle was informed that there was not room for him. His bride however, was allowed to travel, and they arranged to meet at the other side. Frizalle did not cross, but his wife did and it is feared that she is amongst the missing.

ON THE WAY TO DAUGHTER'S DEATH BED

A pathetic feature in connection with the death of Mrs Saunders, of 53, York Road, Kingstown, was that on the previous evening she received a wire from a doctor in England that her daughter was dying. Before going on board the Mail boat she said that she feared impending danger, but owing to her desire to see her daughter she overcame her fear and went on the tragic voyage.

(The Saunders family had more justification than most for unbridled grief and deserve the utmost sympathy for the way with which the sea stole its family members. In 1895 Mrs Saunders' twenty-eight year old husband Francis was drowned whilst crewing the Kingstown lifeboat. On that occasion, all of the volunteer crew of the lifeboat were lost when it capsized during the *Palme* tragedy in Dublin Bay. Even still more sadly, and as the words carved on the tombstone in Dean's Grange cemetery recall, Mrs Saunders' daughter passed away just three days later.)

A sentimental but nonetheless interesting living connection with the *Leinster* tragedy lies with Mrs O. Gray and her husband Shane, who have until recent times operated and lived at their diving instruction centre, 'Scubadive', Coliemore, Dalkey. Mrs Gray's father and grandfather Connolly who both lived at 22 Tivoli Terrace, Kingstown were employed as crew aboard the Leinster when she sank. After they jumped from the sinking ship, they found each other in the water. With the help of Chief Stoker John O'Donohue and Bill Sweeney, also from Kingstown, they were both saved. Later Mrs Gray's father Jack ran a grocery shop in Patrick Street, Kingstown, and while trading there he got the opportunity to buy the company's beautiful mirrored half model of the *Leinster*. He later donated this remarkable exhibit to the Maritime Institute, Haigh Terrace, Dun Laoghaire, Co. Dublin, where it remains today. During the Gray's time at the Coliemore, they have taken many divers to visit the wreck of the *Leinster*.

The final tale of such experiences is not one of sorrow but bravery and good fortune. When the *Leinster* finally disappeared, there were many poor unfortunates injured and adrift in the rough and cold sea. Like Parker's story of tenaciously clinging to a bobbing raft, another similar drama was being enacted nearby. William Maher, a stoker on the Leinster from Desmond Avenue in Kingstown, was desperately clinging to another raft, sharing it with seven others, including Sergeant Duffin. Mrs Louisa Toppin ('Rocklands' at Bulloch, Dalkey), and her twelve year-old daughter Dorothy who had spotted this same raft and made a few strokes to gain its safety. William Maher was unable to haul them aboard the raft but, despite several soldiers clinging to the legs of the Toppins, he was able to hold on to them for another three hours. When a rescue vessel finally reached the raft, there were only four left - the Toppins, Sergeant Duffin and Maher. The crew of the rescue vessel hoisted Duffin and Mrs Toppin aboard, but during the effort Dorothy slipped from Maher's grip. He dived for the sinking girl without success but did so another fourteen times until he recovered Dorothy. All four reached Kingstown safely and William Maher received the Albert Medal for bravery. He also received a beautiful silver watch and chain from Dorothy Toppin with the inscription: 'To William Maher from Dorothy Toppin as a small token of gratitude for saving her life.'

This story was recalled in a brilliant article by Sean Dunne TD in *The Sunday Express* in December 1964 in which he also added a tale of superstition. It has long being believed by fishermen and sailors alike that possession of a thin film of skin called a caul, which is sometimes attached over a baby's head at birth, will prevent drowning. Sean related that both Mrs Toppin and Sergeant Duffin were born with

Dorothy Toppin, daughter of Louisa of Rocklands, Dalkey. Both rescued by William Maher

William Maher, Desmond Ave, Kingstown received the Albert Bravery Medal for the rescue of Louisa and Dorothy Toppin on 10 October

cauls. But William Maher's grandson Liam O'Donovan (his mother was Maher's daughter, Leinster Lily), told me that William himself also had a caul. This seems to lend weight to the superstition when you consider that of the ten on the raft, four grounds of her home 'Rocklands', her body was transported to nearby Bulloch harbour, Dalkey. From there she made that final journey aboard the small fishing launch *Ability* and was laid to rest in Dublin Bay. *The Evening Press* and others recorded the event but no mention was made of her narrow escape from the sea thirty-three years earlier. It was from the sea that she had escaped, but its call was finally answered.

None of the newspaper reports could sufficiently convey the pitiful scenes emanating from the mortuaries and hospitals throughout Dublin after the sinking. Particularly stretched were the staff at St Michael's Hospital, Kingstown, who managed to demonstrate considerable compassion, understanding and care despite acute shortages.

The target for blame was quickly nominated - it was, of course, 'The Murdering Hun'. Tales of past atrocities were added to fuel a new fervour of hate. Blatant inaccuracies such as 'innocent civilians only were aboard' appeared daily without shame. *The Daily Graphic* on 12 October stated that there were '500 lives lost on the *Leinster*' and continued 'only fifteen of the 100 women and children on board the *Leinster* were saved'. These exaggerated headlines of the women and children lost served to pluck at the heart strings but conveniently neglected to mention who the remaining 400 were. There was no mention whatsoever of the extent of the military personnel transported on these vessels in the past or on 10 October. But the *Leinster's* journal clearly reveals in its final entry for that day that '67 military officers and 425 other ranks were aboard the *Leinster* when she was lost, of which 328 were killed'. This entry is signed by the principal director of the CDSPCo., Mr William Watson, and does not differ from the official statistics which were in the possession of the authorities but not published until now.

Germany was accused of 'not playing the war game fairly'. This was the language used by Captain Gwynn MP whose words were reported in *The Freeman's Journal* thus: 'Germany has swept away all the old usages of chivalry and moderation in war'. Captain Gwynn must have been totally removed from the millions of dead, twisted and maimed bodies returning from the bloodiest 'moderate' war in history.

At this time, Germany was making representations for peace with approaches to the Allies. An article appearing in *The Illustrated London News*, attributed to President Wilson, read as follows: 'At the very time that the German Government approaches the Government of the US with proposals of peace, its submarines are engaged in sinking passenger ships at sea, and not the ships alone but the very boats in which their passengers and crews seek to make their way to safety'.

There were two elements to this remark by President Wilson which had some basis in fact, but not in the case of the Leinster nor in the sinking of the *SS Dundalk* which took place a few days later nearer to Holyhead. (This second attack on the *Dundalk* was reported in the newspapers, but some salient facts which might support the view that survivors had more to fear from their own side than from a surfaced U-boat were omitted by the sensor. After the *Dundalk* sank, the attacking U-boat surfaced, but dived again soon after without further incident. Almost immediately afterwards the steamer *SS Carlingford* passed by and those on deck saw the survivors frantically waving and crying out. Instead of coming to their rescue, the ship went astern and steamed on. Later testimonies by the crew of both vessels confirmed this, with the Captain of the *Carlingford* stating that he saw a submarine and steamed on to avoid being attacked.)

The reference to attacks on 'innocent passenger ships' and 'attacking the lifeboats' had been well documented but such monstrous behaviour did not apply in the case of the *Leinster*. Firstly, the majority of the passengers were military, and not only on this occasion but on many previous occasions. Secondly, the *Leinster* often carried military stores. What was a German U-boat commander who left Germany several weeks earlier to do? His orders were to sink enemy ships. Does he stop the ship, remove the civilians and then sink her with just the soldiers and crew aboard? Not very likely. (This remarkable consideration was actually per-formed on a few occasions by German submarine commanders.) And as we've seen, the mail boats were a nominated target.

As for the reference to 'attacks on survivors in open boats', there are recorded incidences of this despicable behaviour by German U-boat commanders. Although this remark may not have been directed at the *Leinster* incident, it nevertheless had some local relevance. Earlier that year it had been reported that some fishing boats had been attacked by a German submarine with the loss of several lives. Although unjustified attacks such as these were utterly cowardly, in some instances these 'fishing boats' were relaying U-boat positions by wireless, which nullified their neutral status. Such was the case in the incident on 25 March 1917, when a German U-boat came alongside the *Arklow Light Vessel*. The commander of the submarine ordered the crew of the lightship into the boats and then sunk it with explosives. This was in retaliation for the crew's role in warning passing convoys and in relaying the submarine's positions to the Admiralty. The U-boat commander did not fire on the defenceless ship and sink it with crew on board, as he very well might have felt entitled to do. In balance, there are also recordings of cowardly attacks on innocent vessels such as 'hospital ships'. These horrible war crimes were committed by U-boat commanders in order to draw away and stretch Allied escorts to the limits of their operations. There was also the sinking of the Japanese liner *Hirano Maru*, off the South coast of Ireland, again with the loss of 'innocent civilians'. Whether or not the fact that chief officials of the London Office of the Yokohama Specie Bank were on board the *Hirano Maru*, or the fact that Japan had joined the fight against Germany and had been supplying the Allies with arms, was of any interest to the general public is unknown, as the latter was not worthy of reporting. But it certainly provides room for further speculation.

Publicity in Germany on the *Leinster* affair (which was controlled) was reported to be not too dissimilar. The Germans always denied giving orders for the sinking of 'innocent passenger ships'. Indeed, they never specifically apologised for torpedoing the *Leinster*. One of the few official comments emanating from Germany on the *Leinster* affair appeared in the *Berlin Telegraph* and was relayed by Reuters: 'Much as the death of civilians not directly participating in the war must be regretted, it must be emphasised in connection to the enemy press agitation, the distinction between a passenger steamer and a transport ship is impossible, just as it is impossible for a British airman to distinguish whether his bombs dropped on Bruges killed German soldiers or Belgium citizens'. In this statement you see no apology for an attack on those who formed the majority of the passengers aboard the *Leinster* but there is regret for the loss of innocent life. This is closer to a balanced statement which was not seen in the Irish or British press, but which, I hope, must have expressed the overall sentiments of both sides.

Another report relayed from a Dutch newspaper records an interview with Minister Erzberger of Germany's Centre Party. Fearing the propagandist reports on the sinking of the *Leinster* during sensitive peace negotiations, he commented: 'I don't hesitate to declare that I consider the tragedy extraordinarily regrettable, and have the deepest sympathy with the innocent women and children. My standpoint has always been the same since the Lusitania, when I publicly expressed my regret about the victims. In this case my regret is most keen. It is high time that all useless suffering inflicted should be stopped.' Again there is only the carefully reported reference to 'innocent women and children'.

There may have been some reason to believe that the German government was regretting the ferocity of the late attacks by their submarine commanders while peace negotiations were in progress. Large portions of territory had been regained by the Allies in Europe which might have reduced the Germans' ability to contact their submarine commanders. This view is supported by the fact that very few submarine attacks occurred outside the waters around Great Britain and Ireland during October.

It is also supported by the following message which was sent to the Foreign Office by decypherer Mr Robertson at The Hague on 12 October: 'I hear from reliable source that German Legation here have telegraphed to Berlin begging them to issue a statement that torpedoing of *Leinster* and Japanese passenger ship have made very painful impression on them and that it was work of old regime with which new regime cannot agree especially as women and children were drowned. Member of Dutch office told me today that he knew that German Admiralty had great difficulty in communicating with their submarines and could not be sure for several weeks that instructions had reached all of them. This came when Dutch coal ships were torpedoed. They were merely promised relative security when they left and absolute security after six weeks. Submarine that sunk them had had her wireless shot away.'

A note below the message read: 'I send above for what it's worth but German legation here is alleged to be pacifist. German naval Attaché under the old regime has been recalled.'

This report confirms that a peace was being negotiated and that some kind of 'new' orders were sent to submarine commanders. But, alas, we do not know that even if those orders had been received by *UB-123* they would have saved the *Leinster*.

It might seem that the *Leinster* could not have been mistaken for anything other than one of the mail steamers. Obviously some commanders had trouble with silhouettes, and given the pictures of her in camouflage and in view of the high speed at which she travelled, it is understandable how any of the mail boats which were similarly presented could have been mistaken for a destroyer. Considering the vast amount of U-boat attacks that occurred, there was only a relatively small number of cowardly commanders who perpetrated acts which could be termed indiscriminate. But war can strip away the veneer and vestiges of man's humanity with no regard for nationality or creed. This was true for these cowardly acts perpetrated during the conflict and they were not confined to one side only.

Disgust and revulsion expressed in the daily newspapers at the growing toll of dead bodies was directed squarely at the 'wicked German enemy' and their 'Irish Nationalist Allies'. This was the type of stuff that was being churned out to fan the flames of conscription. The Foreign Secretary Mr Balfour excelled with a speech on 11 October which contained the following statement: '*The Leinster* was carrying no military stores and serving no military object'. This, of course, was just another downright lie, but he continued eloquently and the extract that follows was widely reported: 'Although the Germans have attempted to change their constitution, they have not changed their hearts. Brutes they were when they commenced the war, and brutes they remain.' In the case of *The Freeman's Journal*, this was rounded off with a contemptuous verse by a frequent contributor to that paper:

The Leinster

Brutes they began the war, and brutes remain.
In blacker hearts was never spawned the seed
Of crime malignant, callous butcher deed.
Nothing can wash the ineffaceable stain,
And long as English letters shall spell plain
'Leinster' and 'Lusitania,' these shall plead
With Christ against the Teuton's pagan creed,
And claim swift justice for our innocent slain.

We wait no judgement morning for the sea
From charnel depths to give us back our dead.
To-day they rise, and cry against the Huns;
And coward shall his name for ever be
Who till our last retribution boldly is sped
Shall stop the avenging thunder of our guns.

H D. Rawnsley, The Abbey, Carlisle

Balfour also included in his speech: 'This Irish packet boat, crammed as it always is, with men, women, and children, in broad daylight, was deliberately torpedoed by a German submarine ... That is only one and not the most destructive, the most cowardly, or the most brutal thing they are perpetrating on helpless civilians or still more helpless prisoners of war'. Without a doubt, it was rising stuff indeed. He went on with emotional pleas to 'avenge your brother or sister' and calls 'upon the honour and manhood of Ireland to assert itself and wreak vengeance on the Prussian Monster'. There could not have been a more timely or opportune piece of recruiting propaganda even if it appeared uncertain whether or not that the war would soon end. Three days after the sinking, the recruiting machine seized at the opportunity and set up at Dalkey and the Town Hall in Kingstown, opposite the Carlisle Pier. Here the spin doctors did their stuff and included another threat: 'Ireland would never get Home Rule until it proved itself a nation'. The enormity of the event did not escape the attention of the Bray Urban Councillors who were forthright in their condemnation in the 19 October issue of the *Bray and South Dublin Herald*. They colourfully blamed 'the dictates of the inhuman Prussian Vampire for the loss of nearly 600 lives'. And again there was no mention of a military presence aboard the vessel.

The issue of the war's end seemed to be a little murky and was not helped by the confusing headlines in the Freeman's Journal on two occasions. On 12 Oct-ober, it recorded Sir Douglas Haig's address to the troops, 'repudiating ill founded rumours that Peace was at hand and urging the troops on to the ultimate and final goal of "total victory"'. Two days later, on 14 October, appeared the headline: 'Germany Admits Defeat'. In New York it was a little clearer for the Chairman of the War Industries Board who called on the American nation to 'Think War, Talk War and Make War'. And, of course, make more money for American munitions manufacturers. If there had been any doubt remaining, the following insertion in the

Freeman's Journal on the conscription question would confirm the danger had passed:

CONSCRIPTION

In view of the intense public interest as to the danger of conscription being applied to Ireland, we are glad to be in a position to state that the chance of any such attempt being made is now practically non-existent.

We earnestly urge upon our people the vital importance of maintaining the attitude of unity, self-restraint, and discipline which up to the present has been crowned with such triumphant success.

The 'dastardly deed' and the recruitment propaganda, all served to portray the Nationalists in a bad light as allies to the 'Murdering Hun' who were slaughtering British people. The trade unions and the Nationalists, grouped together as they often were, condemned outright all acts of violence on innocent civilians. It is true that they got little honest opportunity through the media to defend themselves, their only recourse being illegal leaflets and newsletters. There is a copy of a rare pamphlet in the National Library which contains very interesting criticism on the role of the *Leinster* and the part played by the authorities in the *Leinster* disaster. As the press was censored and propagandist it is important to examine all published material in order to try and extract some kind of balanced view of contemporary opinions.

The pamphlet was headed *The Leinster Outrage* - and quite justifiably. But it was the innocent civilians and their families only who were entitled to deep outrage. Who they should have been outraged at is another matter. The next question on the pamphlet was: 'Why has there been no inquest.' Well, there quite obviously were inquests but maybe not the required ones. As to the reference to 'awkward questions', none were put to any representative of the relevant authorit-ies as they did not attend the inquests. Let's look at the points the pamphlet raises.

Point No. 1
- 'Was the *Leinster* a War Vessel or a Passenger Boat?' The most relevant answer to this question was that the Germans considered her a legitimate target for very good reasons.
- As to the Mail Boat having been recently stopped by a German submarine and warned 'that if it was used as a troop ship it would be sunk', it is true that the *Leinster* had stopped on at least one occasion to 'avoid a sub' but whether or not any communication took place between the two commanders is not known.
- The claim that there was a recent return to daylight sailings is true and for the *Leinster* the following are some of the recorded changes: after being out of service and in dry dock from 29 May to 29 June, daylight sailings resumed. Night sailings were restored again on 9 September with passages of large numbers of troops. They ended and returned to daylight sailings on 2 October. The accusation that there were 500 troops aboard on the Leinster's last trip is extremely close to the number 492 recorded by the CDSPCo.

THE LEINSTER OUTRAGE.

Why has there been no Inquest?
Because awkward questions would be asked

(1) Was the *Leinster* a War Vessel or a Passenger Boat?

The Mail Boat was stopped recently by a German submarine and warned that if used as a troop ship it would be sunk. Hence the change to daylight sailings, notwithstanding which the Government used her to transport soldiers, and there were 500 aboard on her last trip.

(2) The English Army goes down fighting (?)

When the *Leinster* was torpedoed a life-boat full of women and children was rushed by the soldiers and overturned before it left the ship, and every occupant of this boat was drowned. The 500 English soldiers went mad with panic.

(3) Gallant rescue work.

The incident took place a little beyond the Kish Lightship. Almost immediately the Holyhead-Kingstown Mail Boat and a London and North Western Boat steamed through the passengers and debris in the water without stopping, Mr. Shortt being an interested spectator, and although Dublin Bay is full of shipping—patrol boats—it was two hours before any boat arrived to rescue—one hour and a half *to make up their minds* and 20 minutes to get there. The schedule time from Kingstown to Holyhead is $2\frac{3}{4}$ hours for 64 miles. The Kish is 10 miles from Kingstown Harbour !!

A Sinn Féin propaganda leaflet which was produced after the Leinster *disaster. It is notably very accurate*

Point No. 2

This is an attack on the chivalry of the English Army which, of course, had more than just a smattering of Irishmen in its ranks. There was no evidence to support the accusation that the troops were inordinately unchivalrous. Both Captain Cone and the Assistant Purser Bill Sweeney recorded that there was cowardly behaviour by both crew and soldiers during their bid to escape the sinking ship. There was some 'fluffing' by witnesses around this issue at the inquest which resulted in the only official misgiving by the inquest, and that was that 'lifeboat No. 5 made no effort to save life'.

Point No. 3

This addresses the response time to the tragedy which seemed to have been unduly lengthy. The LNWR steamer which 'steamed' through debris and bodies was instructed by the Admiralty to carry on as there were already sufficient boats on the scene. (This vessel was probably the *Galtee More* which left Dublin at 14.15 and was escorted by *HMS Avon*.) There were bodies and debris in the water, but this could only be expected. The response time as experienced by many of the victims in the water seemed longer than it should have been for rescue vessels to reach the scene.

Little more can be said of this pamphlet except that it was obviously anti-British, but it was certainly accurate on many points.

Amid the outpourings of sympathy and grief which filled the daily newspapers there was, as there always is, room for the opportunists. The new uncertainty of travel on the Irish Sea in the public's minds was seized upon and, in an attempt to remind them of their duty and their mortality, insurance companies seized the golden opportunity which presented itself. The following adverts were run in The *Irish Times* and *The Freeman's Journal* on 14 October. This blatant exploitation showed a remarkable lack of sensitivity for many grieving relatives. It was also the only type of compensation which the authorities referred to when asked to compensate the dependants of those lost on the *Leinster*!

Two insurance adverts

Led by the Dublin Corporation, there were many calls for a 'searching enquiry' into the *Leinster affair*, but the only type allowed were inquests and even then, the Admiralty and the War Office would not attend nor answer any questions.

The first and the speediest inquest was held on Mr Shaw Jones, thirty-seven, an auditor for the Ministry of Munitions. The result was short and straightforward, returning a verdict of 'death by drowning'. The second inquest was that on Miss Georgina O'Brien, a clerk who was returning to her employment in London. This was more of a heavyweight affair and commenced one week after the disaster and took one week to complete. Representing the next of kin was the well known Mr Gavan Duffy. For the Attorney General was Mr Henry Hanna KC, and representing the Dublin Steam Packet Co. was Mr Denis Henry KC. Superintendent Flynn and Inspector Kirwan attended on behalf of the Dublin Metropolitan Police.

The mood of the public was one of anger at the Admiralty's refusal to provide escorts, and one of expectancy and revelation from the coroner's enquiries. Not only was the reporting of the inquest heavily censored and edited but the public was further disappointed with the coroner, Mr W.A. Rafferty JP, who never allowed the proceedings to stray onto questions which might prove embarrassing for the Crown. (Unfortunately the record of these court proceedings are missing from the National Archives.) His intention was to determine the actual cause of death and not 'who or what' contributed to it. During the inquest, many members of the travelling public and members of the crew were called to give evidence. They were required to testify on the condition and safety equipment of the ship. They also gave evidence on the events immediately leading up to the attack and were required to answer questions on the Admiralty's role in the rescue operation. Evidence given expelled any doubt as to the 'well found' condition of the ship and supported the fact that all of its safety equipment was in excess of its official requirements. When the ship was launched, it was reported that she was licensed to carry 1,400. (This may have been inaccurate as it did not correspond to a reduced certified figure in Board of Trade records.)

The *Leinster* carried ten lifeboats, but in any of the pictures taken of the *Provinces*, with the exception of the camouflaged mail boat on which eight can easily be seen, only six can be seen. Somewhere in the interim the lifeboats were augmented to ten along with the fitting of a 12 lb gun on the poop deck. Under close inspection, the two smaller lifeboats can be seen just inside the two at the stern. In any depictions of the sinking *Leinster*, there was no gun shown on the poop deck and, in contrast, a large fluttering flag was incorrectly depicted flying from the stern. Evidence subsequently given to the Board of Trade clearly stated that there was no flag flying which was as per Admiralty instructions.

Although there were more than ample life rafts and life jackets, the certification was testified as having been for 770, and according to the ship's journal this number had not been exceeded in previous years. This was not the case with the *Ulster* who had carried as many as 1,277 troops during the Rebellion in 1916. What was also a little unusual was that all of the official tallies on the 'lost' and 'survivors' amounted to within one or two of the figure of 770 - even the last entry in the *Leinster's* journal recorded 771. This means there was either a very well managed ticket system - or equally well managed figures. The only criticism of the ship's lifesaving equipment came again from Captain Cone's report. In it he stated that the life boats should have been rigged out and that some of the other devices were in a poor state of maintenance.

Testimony was given that included evidence of three earlier and recent attacks on the *Leinster* and also on events leading up to and including the attack. All of this evidence appears to have been consistent, with the exception of the wireless message which was purported to have originated from the *Leinster*. There was considerable uncertainty as to who first received this message and at what time. It was generally accepted that the *Ulster*, who had passed the *Leinster* at the Kish at 09.42, received a weak message at 09.50, whilst approaching Kingstown harbour. Despite meticulous entries by the officers in the ship's journals, there was no mention of the incident nor of the wireless message. This may only be because the incident caused no delay or it may be something completely different. The message is stated to have been: 'SOS TORPEDOED' and was relayed by the wireless officer of the *Ulster* at 09.52. The pier master was then informed when the ship docked at 10.18. The Admiralty stated, in reply to Commons' questions, that the *Ulster* received the SOS at 09.25. Unintentionally or otherwise, this admission by the Admiralty only confused the issue. If the *Ulster* had received a message at the premature time of 09.25, why then, when the *Ulster* was only a short distance outside the harbour, would it take until 10.18 for the master of the Ulster to inform the pier master at Kingstown? Under examination from Mr Henry Hanna KC, Lieutenant Commander Dillon from the naval base at Kingstown stated that his patrol boat in the harbour received instructions to 'go out' at 09.58, and did so almost immediately.

What the court did not know, was that the ship's Adjutant, Second Lieutenant H.L. Parker had made a report to his superiors on 11 October which contained the following testimony: '... the ship was hit portside, forward at about 9.37...' He also testified that '... I rushed onto the bridge where I found Captain Birch standing talking to Captain Cone of the US Navy ... I said to Captain Birch "I have come to report Sir, what are your orders?" He [Captain Birch] replied, "Just wait one minute, Mr Parker". He then gave some orders to Captain Cone and turning to me said "The wires are gone, so we have not been able to send a message."' Almost immediately the second torpedo struck and First Officer Crangle was thrown into the water where, he testified, his watch stopped at 09.55. If Lieutenant Parker was correct, the very earliest a message could have been sent would have been 09.38 - but again, if he was correct, no message was sent at all! And certainly no message was sent after the second explosion at between 09.50 and 09.55.

Under oath, no member of the crew, including the most senior surviving officer Crangle, was able to testify that a message was sent. A message was received, so who sent it? Unfortunately the radio officer Arthur Jeffries, who could have thrown some light on this question and who was reported to have remained in the radio room, was killed during the second explosion. Neither Captain Cone's report nor his evidence was recorded as being called upon during the inquest. It is also recounted by Sean Dunne in *The Sunday Express* (16 December 1964), that Paddy Ryan, the wireless operator aboard the *Ulster*, had received a feeble message from the *Leinster*. Captain Robert Newton of the *Ulster* is then reported to have seen the *Leinster* going down through his binoculars, after which he gave the order to Paddy Ryan to send out a general SOS. I have already stated that in spite of meticulous entries in the mailboats' journals, there was no reference in either of them, or by the management of the CDSPCo., to this effect. (The whole SOS question is addressed again later.)

As for the Admiralty's role in the disaster, questioning was confined to its response time to the sinking and its effectiveness in the rescue of survivors. The earliest response from Kingstown was reported to have been by commander Dillon, who received orders to go out at 09.58, but when he arrived on the scene at 10.36, he reported another naval vessel already there. The statements on the response time ranged from less than 40 minutes to 120 minutes. The matter was inconclusive but it was agreed that all speed was made by the Admiralty in getting to the scene. When boats arrived close to the scene, they had to reduce speed in order not to injure those in the water and experienced a lot of difficulty hoisting survivors from the water over the high gunwales of the navy boats in very heavy weather.

Shortly after the opening of the inquest, the proceedings were postponed, but not before Gavan Duffy was reported to have requested all the surviving officers from the *Leinster* as witnesses. This was to include the Radio Officer at Kings-town. Commander Dennison did appear, but there was no report nor mention of testimony from such a radio officer.

As you might expect, there were some heated exchanges between counsel during the proceedings which were a manifestation of the political tensions of the day. There was also some criticism of the jury itself. At one point, Mr Gavan Duffy for the next of kin protested to the jury against the 'action of the Irish Executive'. He accused them as follows: 'that a loyal jury likely to be prepossessed in favour of the crown was selected to hear the evidence'. Mr Hanna for the Attorney General was encouraged to reply: 'that the enquiry was pro German', returning an agitated Duffy to his feet in indignation. Gavan Duffy, aroused once more by the earlier evidence of Mr William Watson (MD of the CDSPCo.) of pleadings to the Admiralty for protection, and the State's absence at the proceedings, continued a scathing attack which ended: 'One fact that stood out above all others was the appalling recklessness, not to say cruelty, of those who allowed the public to take such risks. No plea of war necessities could excuse it. This was the only enquiry which would be held into the disaster, and the jury would not exonerate, by silence, those responsible.'

Not to be outdone, Mr Hanna again rose to his feet accusing Mr Duffy, in an equally long tirade, of using the proceedings as a 'mouthpiece of attack' on the forces of the Crown.

The jury retired and returned four times unable to break a deadlock. The focus of their disagreement was 'censure' of the Admiralty, on which issue the juror Mr Good had a lot to say with none of the narrow focus suggested by Mr Hanna. Mr Duffy also interjected some informative words on Coroners' Law which was met with howls of laughter from the court: 'That if jurymen could not agree in their verdict they were to be kept without meat, drink, or fire until they returned their verdict.' They were then instructed to retire once more and come to conclusions based on the following questions:

1. What was the cause of death?
2. Were all possible means taken to save life by the City of Dublin Steam Packet Co. on board the *Leinster?*
3. Was all that could be done to save life done by the Naval authorities at Kingstown?
4. Do you attach any blame to the responsible authorities in not affording an escort to the *Leinster* on the day of the disaster?

The jury retired and returned without undue delay. But before the verdict was read out, up shot a member of the jury who expressed 'unhappiness' at the censuring of the Admiralty by attributing 'blame' on them in question 4. Earlier, Mr Hanna KC had already expressed that the proceedings were being used as a mouthpiece of attack, but also added at this point that 'these eruptions were designed to demonstrate that the jury was infiltrated with Anti Crown Nationalists'. However, after a further absence by the jury, they agreed and returned the following verdict:

*   In respect of question 1: 'Drowning'.
*   In respect of questions 2, 3 and 4: 'Yes'.

The jury also expressed the opinion that the most regrettable incident of the disaster was that 'There was no evidence to show that No. 5 lifeboat made any effort to save life'.

For the fourth question, it meant that the Admiralty was censured for not providing adequate protection for the *Leinster*, but was credited for responding to the disaster promptly and, in so doing, saved life.

As we saw earlier, escorts were only provided at the discretion of the Admiralty. It may not have mattered at all, but an airship was damaged while landing at Malahide on the day previous to the sinking. Would it have been provided for escort otherwise? Unlikely. There was also the item of the patrolling drifter lost some weeks earlier and the submarine attacks and sightings in the Irish Sea within the previous twenty-four hours. There were repeated questions in Parliament on the question of escorts and the delay in arrivals at the scene. Despite repeated accusations and examples of similar cases where steamers received escorts, the Admiralty always maintained the view that the *Provinces'* superior speed provided their best defence against attack, and that escorts could not hope to keep up. This sounds plausible enough, but the patrol boat which was alongside in Kingstown harbour and received orders at 09.58 to 'go out' actually went faster than the *Leinster* did in reaching the same position. That is, according to the Admiralty, the destroyer achieved the distance in thirty-eight minutes whereas it took the *Leinster* 'at best' an estimated forty-three minutes.

The criticisms amounted to nothing, but escorts were provided immediately thereafter. There was, of course, no problem 'keeping up' with the mail steamers following the disaster (only *two Provinces* remained), and there never had been with the *Connaught* when she was lost conveying troops in the English Channel. The fact was that all innovations and methods were belatedly employed to protect the remaining *Provinces*, including fast destroyers that could do in excess of twenty knots. When these were not available, the Admiralty used relays of vessels over shorter distances and extensive patrols from the air.

This was an issue to which Edward Watson referred when he addressed the half-yearly meeting of the Board of the CDSPCo. in November. He complained that some of the evidence which he had given at the inquest had been suppressed, and also pointed out that destroyers had no problem 'keeping up', either before or after the incident. He also confirmed that it was Captain Birch on the *Leinster* 'who had the greatest number of escapes'. In addition, he gave an explanation for the increase in life preserving measures aboard the *Leinster*. This, he explained, was a result of requests by the BOT who had promised 'that on completion they would assist the company in their petitions for escorts'. But alas, the promises once more proved empty.

Let's return to the question of why the *Leinster* was chosen as a target. This vessel was seen as the proud flagship of the fleet. Crossing in her was almost a social occasion - a journey to relish, during which like-minded people could be entertained with pleasant and witty conversation by the notable Captain and his crew. This vessel reported in *The Nation* as 'the famous Irish Channel passenger boat' carried dozens of high ranking officers and noblemen. Only two days before the sinking, King Manoel, the recently abdicated King of Portugal, crossed in her. (His return was scheduled for the next day but was fortunately postponed by the timely invitation by Lady Arnot to a dinner party at Merrion Square.) But why did the *Leinster* have so many admirers? One simple explanation is that it was not just the *Leinster* but any of one of these steamers that had eluded by their turn of speed, and probably also their clever camouflage paintwork, the many attempts to sink them. When they carried large numbers of troops or distinguished passengers they quite often were escorted. So you could say that the odds, if not more favourable on a safe mail boat crossing, were at least more exciting.

Are these reasons sufficient for the *Leinster* receiving so much mention? The popularity of the *Leinster* with the public - and U-boat commanders - was apparently well known. It was reported in a tribute to Captain Birch in the *Nautical Magazine* 1918 that 'the Huns had been watching for the Leinster and that Commander Birch knew it well enough'. This obsession with the Leinster is also confirmed by reports from the shores of Wales. Shortly after the sinking, a reporter interviewed a director of the CDSPCo. at Holyhead who had been aboard the *Leinster*. He revealed to the journalist an awareness that the company and the Admiralty possessed. Among his indignant remarks were the following: 'For a long time past we have been aware that the Huns were determined to get the *Leinster*.' He also claimed that *'The Leinster* was the largest and fastest of the boats'. These are both very unusual statements to make. The first begs the question as to how the Huns could distinguish the *Leinster* and why they especially wanted to sink her. The second, and its reference to size and speed, is also a mystery. Although the mail steamers were identical in construction, it is understandable how over years of operation one could become faster than the other. But it is difficult to understand how, without some alterations, the *Leinster* could have been bigger than the others. But if it was, it would explain huge increases in the amount of mail and parcel baskets which it carried.

Originally built to accommodate up to 250 mail sacks, this figure was seldom if ever reached prior to the War, and little consideration could be given to the small number of parcel baskets that were conveyed. But as you might expect, these figures steadily rose during the war years and finally reached an all time high for the *Leinster* in 1918. On 6 October, it recorded 635 parcel post baskets. These figures were well in excess of the specifications on which the ship was originally ordered and built. Here may be a clue to the earlier mystery of 'shutting out' at 650 passengers, suggesting that alterations to the original parcel post accommodation had being carried out during the intervening years.

The Welsh *Chronicle* seemed to have been less affected by the censor than Irish newspapers. For instance, it had no problem mentioning some of the more prominent officers killed and their subsequent burials. Nevertheless, the large number of soldiers aboard and lost was not revealed here either. The *Chronicle* was less restrictive in its reporting of subsequent debates in the House of Commons, covering many interesting aspects of the disaster. It recorded that in a debate on Monday 21 October, Lord Oranmore and Browne who had crossed on the *Leinster* just two days before the sinking was informed by an official also aboard, that an attempt had been made on the *Leinster* the previous day (i.e., 9 October). He also said that 'if the Kingstown and Holyhead route could not be properly protected, then women and children should not be permitted by the route'. This was a key admission and the nub of the authorities' guilt in the affair. The same issue of the *Chronicle* reported on a subsequent Commons debate on Wednesday 23 October. This debate concerned itself with the conflicting transmission times of radio messages, the viability of the Kingstown wireless station and the subsequent rescue delays. The East Mayo Nationalist representative, Mr Dillon, seemed to have realised a point which eluded others when he questioned the Secretary to the Admiralty thus: 'Is it possible that the senior naval officer at Kingstown in his report did not give full details as to whether the wireless message was received direct from the *Leinster* or from another vessel'.

The *Chronicle* of Friday 11 October ran an article which included 'Latest details' from their correspondent in Holyhead. He quoted 'a rumour prevalent right along the North Wales coast last night that the vessel was lost with all hands'. This was reported to have been updated later in the day with 'all lives had been saved'. The only difference between this report and the offending one (which was to appear in the *Evening Herald* and was reported on in *The Independent*), was that in the *Chronicle* it was a '*rumour*' and in the *Herald* it was as an 'official report'. The *Chronicle* of 18 October revealed many more tales, with a comprehensive full page spread on page four. This issue includes an account of a conversation between a representative of the paper and a survivor who was interviewed in a Dublin hotel and stated that: 'We [those in his lifeboat] were told that only one wireless message could be got off before the aerials and the installation gave way'. He also went on to describe the help which arrived: 'This was a destroyer, which had picked up our SOS miles away from where we were sunk'.

Inevitable and exasperating questions just keep arising. Who gave this survivor such detailed information? All the officers were on the bridge after the first torpedo, but the only recorded reference to a message or aerials was Captain Birch's conversation with Parker when he said none was sent. Captain Birch was with

Captain Cone, Crangle knew nothing of a message and the remaining Second, Third and Radio officers were killed. It also appears that the first rescue boat on the scene was not from Kingstown, but was the destroyer, *HMS Mallard*, which was on patrol some miles away with *HMS Seal*.

The American newspapers added nothing to what has already gone except that the *New York Herald*, like the English Daily Graphic, upped the death toll to 600. Also, like the *Graphic*, it produced the elusively disguised toll numbers: '135 women and children die' making no mention of the identity of the other 465 claimed to have perished. Again, the disaster was compared to the Lusitania but it received remarkably less press attention. An article in the *New York Herald* on 13 October expressed itself pretty much in agreement with the British papers, commenting on the 'wanton and destructive attack on the mail ship *Leinster*'. It continued thus: 'The *Leinster* affair is seen less excusable than the destruction of the Lusitania since there can have been no possible suspicion on Germany's part that she was carrying war materials of any kind. If, also, any thought was entertained that Germany has been tender on account of the Irish feeling, it is removed by the *Leinster* tragedy'.

I have demonstrated clearly the clandestine role of these mail boats, but it is quite frustrating to witness the contrived interpretation of 'war material' expounded in the media. Surely the public could see through this ruse. But then, maybe only those who travelled on the mail boats knew what they carried.

Finally, the sinking of the *Leinster* precipitated, and was probably in part responsible for, three important developments. Firstly, the Admiralty provided escorts until the danger subsided. Secondly, and maybe more importantly, it was announced in the *Chronicle* on 25 October that 'from October 10th. Merchant Service officers are entitled to 14 days leave with full pay'. Lastly, and a little less useful, on 25 October the Board of Trade promised the relatives of all merchant seamen who lost their lives by torpedo attack a "Torpedo Badge".'

By the time the second inquest concluded, all of the principle church services were ended. Cathedrals and churches were thronged with civic and religious dignitaries, accompanied by thousands of mourners throughout the country. Well in excess of £100,000 had been collected from various counties, co-ordinated at The Mansion House. Major contributors to the fund were the theatres throughout the country who ran benefit performances from which all of the proceeds were donated. What the final amount was and how it was distributed (did it go to military and civilian sufferers evenly, for example?) I do not know.

The war ended one month after the attack on the *Leinster*. At best, given the repeated attempts and encounters by the mail boats with U-boats, the Authorities were negligent in not providing adequate protection. At worst, it was a despicable disregard for public safety, given the knowledge that so many troops were allowed to mix with innocent and unsuspecting travellers on the route. If one were sceptical enough, it might be appropriate to consider the circumstances and accusations that were similar to those in the case of the *Lusitania*. A dastardly attempt at maybe 'setting up' the *Leinster* for instance? However, the attack has been described recently by a USN archivist as 'a routine U-boat attack' and this, I suspect, is closer to the truth.

Notwithstanding all the evidence in support of a measure of recklessness by the

Authorities in not providing an escort for a legitimate war target, they never relented in their refusal to compensate those civilians who lost relatives or property in the attack. The CDSPCo. was never able to obtain permission to replace the *Connaught* in time and replacement for the Leinster was also put on an equally 'long finger'.

The SOS

The final transmissions of doomed ships never fail to capture the curiosity of historians and casual readers the world over. There is an obsession to understand what exact circumstances prevailed during the last moments of a catastrophe and what was going through the wireless operator's mind during his last opportunity to call for help. All readers harbour a faint hope that maybe they will somehow understand or see something in a few words that others have missed.

From the radio officer's point of view, his dilemma is not a comfortable responsibility. He knows that the vessel will probably be lost and that the lives of hundreds of people are depending on his experience and cool headedness. He is faced with sending the message he hoped he would never have to - a moment that his whole career has prepared him for. He has to rely on a steady hand and his ability to send an accurate and recognisable message in order that rescue can be effected. An experienced officer is also well aware that the sea can lose its attractiveness very quickly when you are struggling in it with large waves and the bitter cold, especially if you know that nobody ashore is aware of your predicament.

Such was the case with Arthur Jeffries. He was an experienced radio officer with the CDSPCo. and had come through all the dangers of four years of a determined U-boat campaign in the Irish Sea. It is well accepted that he died in the radio room whilst trying to send a message of distress and for this he will always be well remembered and revered. Some question did arise in relation to the last message from the *Leinster* which I have alluded to earlier. If it was not Jeffries who had sent the first message that was received, could it possibly have been the U-boat?

Given the following diary of transmissions and events, this is probably fanciful, but it has always remained a possibility if only because the origins of that crucial message were never attributed to a sender without any doubt.

Records of the radio transmission

09.42: Log entry from *HMS Mallard:* Received SOS from *RMS Leinster.*

09.50: Log entry *HMS Seal*: Increased rev. to 200. En route to pos. of Leinster. Torpedoed.

09.50: Log entry *HMS Lively*: Received signal *SS Leinster* torpedoed SE of Kish.

These were the three principal ships involved in the aftermath of the sinking, and it was not until Admiral Bayly noticed in Parker's report that Captain Birch had told him that the wires were gone and a message was not sent, that he became curious. He subsequently wrote to the Secretary of the Admiralty and, among other items, he addressed the issue thus: 'This goes to prove that the original SOS was not sent by

Leinster, (I am trying to find out what ship it was) consequently there must have been a delay in the original sending'.

Admiral Bayly sent enquiries to all ships and wireless stations in an effort to clear up this mystery. The replies below are just a few of these, and they help to explain what the series of events were, but they do not confirm who sent the earliest transmission.

A record of entries in the radio log of HMS Lively

09.46: TO KINGSTOWN. from ULSTER - LEINSTER TO - ('PATROL JAMBING) [*this was HMS Patrol*]

09.50: 'LIVELY' from 'KINGSTOWN', Not received SOS - go on. (fragments) - ed LEINSTER TOR LES SE KISH (Interference) SOS from any British Warship - repeat all before two. Kingstown from Ulster. - SOS torpe LEINSTER (shaky sending) torpedoed 2 miles S.E. Kish Lightship.

The above record of transmissions and interceptions by *HMS Lively* were clarified further in a report by the radio officer of the wireless station at Kingstown and is shortened as follows:

Record of entries by the radio officer of the Kingstown wireless station

09.44: The first SOS was heard by me. *HMS Patrol* and Pembroke W/T were working at the same time.

09.46: *HMS Lively* asked Kingstown if we had the SOS from the Ulster. I replied 'NO' and told him to go. As soon as I had finished transmitting I heard the Ulster again sending SOS ...

09.50: Told *Ulster* to repeat and complete message.

There were additional entries but they only confirm that the Ulster was sending an SOS. But was there a transmission earlier than that? Yes, there was and it appears that the *Ulster may* have been the only one to have received it.

After the *Ulster* was enquired from, Commodore Denison made two reports based on the replies he received from the Ulster and from Commander Baggot who was an intelligence officer at Kingstown who had been a passenger on the *Leinster.*

First reply

(A) **09.33:** Captain of *Ulster* reported passing the *Leinster.* Soon after she was struck by first torpedo.

(B) *Leinster's* wireless probably broken down she may have used her emergency set as nothing was heard. (This was the only reference that was ever made to an emergency wireless set.)

(C) **09.44:** Message only partially received owing to interference. (This could have been Kingstown W/T station.) Made by *RMS Ulster*. 09.50: Correct message received.

(D) **09.50:** Message received was made by *RMS Ulster*. No messages were received at Kingstown from *Leinster*.

Although it is not recorded in the *Ulster's* journal, nor any reference made later to it by officials of the CDSPCo., the *Ulster* is undisputedly credited with transmitting an SOS on behalf of the *Leinster*: 'torpedoed 2 miles SE of the Kish Light vessel.' How did the *Ulster* become aware of these facts?

The next reply by Commodore Denison sheds more light on the *Ulster's* part in the exchange of communications.

Second reply
The following details have been received from Captain of *Ulster* who was within a mile of *Leinster* when first torpedo hit.

(begins) Saw *Leinster* alter course suddenly to SSW at 09.37 approximately and go down by head. Asked wireless office if anything wrong with *Leinster*. Operator could hear nothing. On being asked again operator said he could hear very faintly '*Leinster* torpedoed'.

This signal could not have been received by wireless station as it was too weak. *Ulster* then sent out SOS signal at Kingstown.

Starboard ARIEL of *Leinster* was carried away by first explosion which would account for this. (ends)

This report seems to have satisfied all enquiries but, apart from some acceptable exaggerations, I find it inadequate and it raises some further questions. How was the Captain of the Ulster to know that a starboard aerial on the *Leinster* was gone at the time, particularly when none of the officers - nor indeed anybody on board the *Leinster* - was later able to testify to this? (All censorship aside.)
Were '*Leinster* torpedoed' the only faint words that were received by the Ulster and, if so, how was it known that the Leinster sent them?
As the Captain of the *Ulster* was watching the Leinster sink, did he - or did they all - just presume that it was the *Leinster* which was sending the message?

The conclusion I am reaching is that the U-boat sent the message. As much as I would like to think that Commander Ramm had a large measure of compassion in him, to come to such a conclusion, the following circumstances would have to have been the case:

- Firstly, *UB 123* would have to have surfaced between the first and second strike to make the transmission and it would almost certainly have been seen. (U-boats were familiar with the extent of the patrols in this area and it is extremely unlikely they would have risked detection and the loss of boat and crew.)

- Secondly, Commander Ramm could have made his heroic deed known later and there is no suggestion anywhere of this.

What do you think?

You may find it curious that the Ulster (or any other vessel for that matter) which was in sight of the sinking Leinster, and possessed superior speed, did not rush to the scene. These Captains were always under strict instructions by the Admiralty and were bound by *War Instructions for British Merchant Ships* (one of the confidential weighted books in every Captain's possession). In War Instructions, in the chapter dealing with 'Procedures with Regard to Rendering Assistance to Vessels in Distress', lies the answer. It reads: 'Whenever the distress signal for a vessel torpedoed or mined is heard, the locality the signal comes from is to be avoided'.

Two years after the *Leinster affair*, the Chief Censor at the Admiralty during the war, Rear Admiral Sir Douglas Browning, published *Indiscretions of the Naval Censor.* The very last sentence in this book reads: 'P.S. I wish I could have told the whole truth!'

Chapter 7
Lest we forget

Once the news of the Leinster's fate reached the shore staff at Kingstown harbour, it swept through the town. Kingstown is often described today as having 'West British' pretensions, due to its extensive Victorian sea frontage with streets and parks commemorating long forgotten nobility and colonial exploits. Names like Trafalgar, York, Belgrave, Sussex and Mulgrave are found. The town's main street and harbour are named after the landing of King George IV there in 1821. But interspersed with these great names, and removed from the more prominent road frontage, are the little local authority dwellings on Desmond Avenue, Library Road and the Eden Villas of Glasthule. It was from these areas that many of the crew and relatives hailed; many of their fellows came from equally humble dwellings at Holyhead. Consequently it was these places that suffered most, and it was relatives from these areas who reached the Victoria Wharf at Kingstown's harbour first in search of news.

When they arrived, they found access to the quay restricted to medical personnel only and the quay 'strongly held by marines and military'. The crowd grew and clambered outside the perimeter, expressing to one another comforting comments as to the unlikelihood of any serious loss from aboard a mail steamer! It took several hours before the first bodies of victims were brought ashore at 13.30. After this, the rescue vessels were busy with their deliveries back and forth for the remainder of the day. Some of the bodies were laid out in a temporary mortuary on the Carlisle Pier, but were eventually transported to the City Morgue and various hospitals for identification, such as St Michael's Hospital, Kingstown, the Red Cross Hospital at Dublin Castle, King George V (Bricins Military) Hospital, the Rest Camp at North Union (now St James) and so many others. Tragic figures waited for hours and hours in the hope that their loved ones might be aboard the next rescue vessel. There were many disappointed and broken hearted families at the quayside in Kingstown that day.

Survivors were cared for with the greatest of sympathy in such places as the Royal Marine Hotel and the Sailors' Rest Homes in Kingstown and Dublin. The CDSPCo. also made instant arrangements with several seafront hoteliers to accommodate survivors. Great kindness was also shown by many of the local inhabitants.

Compounding the difficulties in getting the survivors into hospitals was the severe lack of beds and medical personnel that the nation was experiencing as a result of the remarkable 'flu epidemic' which was then reaching a climax. Following a milder outbreak in the summer of 1917, this mysterious flu began a ferocious and indiscriminate attack on populations throughout the world in late September 1918. The symptoms were chill, pains throughout and nausea developing into pneumonia. Attending an early victim, a busy doctor told an *Evening Herald* reporter: 'There is no cause for alarm, just take proper reasonable precautions'. The small and insignificant reports continued but escalated with alarming commentary: 'Still spreading', 'Epidemic', 'Flu everywhere' and 'Mysterious malady'. It is extremely moving to read the accounts of this flu which were heralded with comments such as 'no concern' but soon became a 'Raging epidemic'. The treatment suggested was often pathetic: 'Keep in the sun'; 'Go to bed and keep cheerful' - pretty tall orders for a country healing its wounds after a monstrous war during an Irish October.

Headline from The Evening Herald *of 28 October 1918*

It was almost impossible to comprehend the figures being released: 'Hundreds buried in Glasnevin every week'; '1700 in Vienna'; '800 per day in Bombay'; 'In Kimberly, South Africa over 4,000 in the past week'. It was as if the Four Horsemen of the Apocalypse had been unleashed on the world. Many people still recall families been 'taken by the flu' or, as it was sometimes reported, 'The Spanish Flu'. Curiously, people remember in Dublin that the dwellings situated around the slaughter house - 'O'Keefes the Knackers' - in the Liberties for some strange reason seemed to escape the effects of the flu. This pandemic is the worst on record and claimed 19,000,000 lives, with contemporary sources putting it as high as 30,000,000.

Late in the year, a small medical practice in England reported that it had successfully treated patients who showed symptoms of 'Swine Flu', which was believed to have been contracted from infected bacon. But no more than that. It was later suspected that returning soldiers carried the disease, but either the medical authorities did not know this for they did not say, or if they did know it was not reported. But it is now believed by some experts that this disease was indeed Swine Flu. It is conjectured that it was contracted from either horses or mules which were shipped from all over the world for transportation work during the war. The USA was extremely hard hit by this mysterious illness and figures rose to an alarming 2,700 deaths per week in Washington. The situation became so critical that a breakdown in public order was imminent.

Throughout the world the medical profession was urgently in search of a vaccine. The USA finally developed 'a cure', but after nearly 2,000 were inoculated it was discovered that the disease had been misdiagnosed and so the vaccine was useless. However, as mysteriously as it came, this global malady suddenly disappeared of its own volition, leaving a positive source of its origin a mystery. The ramifications of such diseases being passed from animals to humans presents mankind with a haunting spectre to this day.

Kingstown, as all port towns and cities, was badly affected and as if matters could not have been worse, there were several members of the medical profession already locked up for their Nationalist 'sympathies'. All public life was affected and the Dublin Corporation appealed to the authorities for some discretion in their release. I cannot say they were listened to.

The lost crews

A list of all the crew members who died is given in Appendix 1.

The remains of the deceased victims were buried in many local cemeteries - Monkstown, Dean's Grange and the like. But remaining consistent throughout the outpourings of sorrow was the absence of any mention of the large contingent of military lost on the *Leinster*. Lest these poor souls also be forgotten, these victims were buried on the winding Blackhorse Avenue near to Dublin's Phoenix Park. This graveyard, which is relatively obscure, is known as the Grangegorman Military Cemetery. Within the grounds there is a very large cenotaph erected in memory of the merchant seamen who lost their lives in the two Great Wars. A little bit more obscure, unless of course you are looking for them, are the nearby rows and rows of small but neatly erected headstones on the graves of the brave soldiers who also perished aboard the *Leinster*.

The final entry in the *Leinster's* journal reads as below. I have added the final column:

	On board	Survived	Killed
Captain	1	0	1
Crew	76	40	36
Gunners	3	1	2
PO Staff	22	1	21
Military officers	67	34	33
Other ranks	422	129	293
Civilians	180	65	115
Totals	**771**	**270**	**501**

The extensive military list which I have included was an official one which was not published, and it is probably incomplete to only a small degree. It gives some idea of the scale and extent of the military who perished. There were many regiments and nationalities represented, such as Australians, New Zealanders, Canadians, Americans, Irish and English. Many who were saved from the water suffered in hospitals and later died from their injuries. Many hailed from military bases throughout Ireland such as Naval, RAF, USN and obscure bases such as the USA Chemical Warfare School.

The headstones of the soldiers buried in Grangegorman cemetery are of a universal design. Although the design is economic, many are inscribed with the parting sentiments of their loved ones. One modest little verse which drew my attention seems to sum up all the bitterness and waste at the irreplaceable loss of a treasure in a dear young son. It is a sentiment which many a mother must have felt, especially so close to the end of a bloody and horrible war. It reads:

The Cup Was Bitter
The Sting Severe
To Part With Him
We Loved So Dear

May all those young soldiers also rest in peace.

All of eighty years have passed since the Leinster tragedy, but despite another World War, there has never been another incident in Irish waters to equal the tragic loss of the Leinster. The ferry *St Patrick* from Rosslare to Pembroke was bombed in 1941 and the *Princess Victoria* from Larne to Stranraer was lost in the great storm of 1953 - but both of these together did not claim a third of the number of lives lost on the *Leinster*. Over the years there have been a great many shipwreck tragedies in the Irish Sea but none have matched the scale of the *Leinster* tragedy. The *Tayleur* at Lambay Island, Dublin in 1854 and the Pomona at Wexford in 1859 both claimed the lives of more than 400 emigrants.

The town's name and its harbour have long since been changed back again from Kingstown to Dun Laoghaire. The harbour is lined with yacht clubs and pleasure boats and the latest advanced high speed ferries dock at a new terminal, which is where the Victoria Wharf was situated. For now, the old Carlisle Pier still remains for the slower displacement traffic, but even for it, the winds of change are whistling through the old sheds. The City of Dublin Steam Packet Company and its follower B & I are both long gone also. The charming granite Sailor's Rest or Reading Rooms have also been removed for harbour improvements. The principal ferry operator, the Swedish owned Stena Sealink, employs mostly British crew and the tradition of providing crews from the harbour area has all but ended. All these things have gone but the memories of the disaster and the tradition that the mail boats established still survive and live on with the descendants at Dun Laoghaire.

At the time of the *Leinster's* loss, most British merchant ships were insured and underwritten by the British government under a war risk policy. This meant that the *Leinster's* loss was ultimately and eventually compensated for by the British government. Such vessels as those lost because of the war then became the property of the government. In the interim years, the rights to these vessels were sometimes purchased from the British government in order to salvage valuable cargoes and machinery from them. This was the case with the *Leinster,* although not for that reason, when the notable underwater archaeologist Sydney Wignal purchased the wreck. Wignal passed his ownership of the wreck to the present owner, a colleague and fellow historian, Mr Desmond Brannigan, a native of Dublin.

The remains of the military victims of the Leinster being laid to rest at Grangegorman Military Cemetery, Blackhorse Avenue. The pictures depict the burial in 1918 and the scene as it is today

The wreck of the *Leinster*

Because of the distance from the coast to the wreck of the *Leinster* - twelve miles - it has remained over the years generally inaccessible. That is, until recent times. With the onset of modern scuba diving and satellite navigation equipment, the wreck has become easy to locate and a growing source of curiosity and interest for many sport divers. Although the owner has graciously given many divers, including myself, permission to visit the remains, diving on this wreck has often been controversial. In 1991, the present owner resorted to the courts in order to prevent indiscriminate diving to protect the wreck. The incident was reported in *The Irish Times* under the heading of 'Shipwreck trespass case adjourned': 'An application to stop the trespass on or near the wreck of the mail ship *Leinster*, sunk off the east coast in 1918, will be considered in the High Court in Dublin next Monday ... The application was on behalf of Mr Desmond Brannigan, a retired salvage expert, trading as Marine Research, Ballsbridge Terrace, Ballsbridge.'

The case continued for a number of days during which Mr Brannigan established his ownership, recovered artefacts removed from the wreck and successfully obtained an order preventing further trespass on the wreck.

Through the years, there have been many tales and rumours of 'finds' in the wreck of the *Leinster* - artillery shells, diamond rings and all manner of ship's furniture figure in the reports. The most interesting is the claim that, much to a diver's surprise, a number of gold ingots were recovered from some baggage. This would not be surprising as there was a high demand for, and a very brisk trade in, reduced gold and silver for export to Britain. (Curiously, this may have been the ultimate fate of the Irish Crown Jewels which were stolen from Dublin Castle in 1907 and never recovered.)

In order to help the reader appreciate what the wreck is now like, it may be helpful to describe one of these excursions to the site. The boats which sport divers use today are so well developed that a journey to the Leinster can take as little as ten minutes, but more generally it takes about twenty. When the dive boat leaves the confines of Dun Laoghaire harbour there is no need for the shallow draft craft to steer round the Burford or Kish Banks, but it can just head directly for the wreck. Nevertheless, the course passes quite close to the Kish Lighthouse which replaced the light vessel in 1965. This is a large white concrete structure, situated a little nearer to the Kish Bank and often visible from the shore. The lighthouse not only indicates an approach to Dublin, but principally marks the beginning of a long chain of very shallow sandbanks that run parallel to the east coast. These banks have various localised names as they proceed southwards and have been the graves for hundreds - or perhaps thousands - of sail and steam ships down through the years. The five mile journey from the Kish to the wreck of the *Leinster* barely takes another eight minutes before the seabed is being viewed through a 'fish finder' in search of the wreck.

The seabed in the area of the shipwreck has a general depth which does not exceed thirty-three metres. The bottom is sandy and diving must take place during the slackest period of the tide, i.e., just before the flow or ebb, otherwise the strong tidal currents will prove too uncomfortable for even the most experienced. When you first catch a glimpse of the wreck through the often murky waters, the overriding impression is surprise at the extent of the remains and the vast amounts of fish life on it. It is silted up with sand to within three metres of the gunwales, with the top row of portholes protruding from the sand. This picture may change from year to year as the shifting sands come and go. The hull amidships seems to have maintained its integrity but, as you might expect, the centre section is devoid of any deck houses. The bow is practically separated from the main body of the wreck and is twisted well over to port. The stern section is also well silted over and for some reason appears to be badly damaged. The owner suggests that this may have been caused by some very early salvage work. Apart from the damage to the port bow and contents from what was obviously luggage having spilled out in this area, there is little to indicate the extent of the terrible tragedy which occurred on the ship.

This broken jar lay in the wreck face down for eighty years. When turned over, it revealed the classic company's crest in perfect condition

The owner, Des Brannigan, once a seafarer himself, had long held the ambition to have the tragedy and the victims remembered by the town in some appropriate way. His ambition was realised in 1996 when he asked a group of divers to recover one of the *Leinster's* anchors. After many dives, they severed the chain from the starboard anchor and, with great difficulty, recovered it to Dun Laoghaire harbour.

With the help of the local authority, Sealink and the harbour authority, it was unveiled and presented to the public on the promenade opposite the Carlisle Pier.

For those who take the time to read the accompanying plaque, they will find a fitting reminder of the tragic event. And in some similar way, I hope this book will not only recall the dreadful loss of innocent lives, but so too, remind us of our proud maritime traditions and all those merchant seamen who risked their lives daily during those dangerous years in pursuit of that tradition.

The Leinster's *anchor being raised by its owner Desmond Brannigan and local divers*

Bill Sweeney's Interview

In 1912, at the age of sixteen, William Sweeney's father died. He had been employed with the CDSPCo. for over forty years and, as was the tradition within the company, his son was called to take his place. He started as a Junior Clerk at the North Wall for six shillings per week and was appointed as Assistant Purser on the *Leinster* in 1916. He served on the *Leinster* with Captain Birch until it was lost in 1918. During his twilight years he gave a taped interview at Roebuck Home in 1979 in which he recounted his life. It contained rich and sometimes humorous recollections of the times and also a remarkably vivid account of his experiences on the mail boats.

You will notice that Bill Sweeney's name was hardly mentioned and indeed I at first imagined a mistake when I heard mention of him. I subsequently unearthed the tapes of the interview - it's an extensive one and for that reason is not

135

transcribed here in its entirety. I have used it in an isolated way for several reasons. Firstly, it came to me after the book was completed and, to do it justice, I wanted to avoid just slotting in various remarks. Secondly, the interview was held some sixty years after the sinking of the *Leinster* and it might have been said that these recollections were inaccurate. The reader will see from what I have included of his remarks that his recollections were extremely accurate and even more, he is able to give us some valuable insights into the sinking which were not originally made public. Although Bill Sweeney received the 'Torpedo Badge', his dogged and persistent rescue of an unknown Northumberland soldier has, like himself, faded into obscurity. I regret not having made the acquaintance of a man who had such a charming sense of humour and none too little of a boyish impishness for mischief. God bless Bill Sweeney and may he receive a more Heavenly reward.

The person on the left is Assistant Purser William Sweeney. On the right is possibly Hugh Rolands, who drowned. The photo was taken alongside the officers' quarters on the starboard side of the Leinster

In the following interview, Ivr denotes the interviewer and BS Bill Sweeney.

Ivr: Were you inbound or outbound to Holyhead?
BS: We were going out to Holyhead. We had 773 passengers and that included Post Office staff and crew and passengers.
Ivr: And you had some troops aboard?
BS: Oh, stacks of them. That wasn't allowed to be mentioned at the enquiry. It was given information to the enemy.

Ivr: Who was the skipper of the ship at the time?
BS: William Birch, Captain William Birch.
Ivr: And you were Assistant Purser?
BS: Yes.
Ivr: What was it like that morning before the torpedoing?
BS: Well there was a bit of a swell on but you wouldn't say it was dirty weather.
Ivr: Can you tell me tell me if an SOS was sent out?
BS: Yes. I was telling you when they passed each other on the morning sometimes they were very close together. But that particular morning I never seen the other boat so far North. She seemed to be hugging the coastline at Howth.
Ivr: Was this the Ulster?
BS: Yes. She was going into Kingstown. And there was a Mr Adshead on board. He was the manager of the old British Railway, that is the old English Midland Railway. He was their Irish manager. And he said to me, 'Is that the other mail boat over there?' It was so hard to find her. I said, 'Yes'. Poor Adshead, he was drowned.
Ivr: Was it customary to exchange compliments?
BS: Just a tap on the key. That was their 'Good Morning'.
Ivr: Did you ever see the radio officer?
BS: Our radio officer was Jeffries, a Yorkshireman, and the Ulster's radio chap was Paddy Ryan from Tipperary. He was a great character.
Ivr: Where were you on the ship when the torpedo struck?
BS: I was down in the saloon corridor. One of the stewardesses was there. Louise Parry. I had lent her my watch the night before. It had a luminous dial and saved switching on the lights. She could have a look at the time without disturbing the sleeping passengers. We used to sleep so many aboard at night, save having them get up early in the morning and dash down to the boat. But she said, 'Wait a minute Bill, I'll give you your watch back,'as she put her hand in her apron pocket. 'Ah' says I 'I'll be back for it in a second, I've got a call to make.' I had only gone a few yards when I heard this almighty crash and a shattering of glass. I looked into the saloon just before I went up the stairs and the whole mantelpiece over the fireplace was falling down. I didn't know what it was. I got up on deck and Addison, the second mate, he shouted to me, 'We've been torpedoed'. He'd been torpedoed in the Connaught, the sister ship of this one some months before in the English Channel. I went up to the chief officer's room, he always kept a lifebelt under his chair. But there wasn't any there. Somebody had got there before me. So I wasn't going down to my room to look for one. There was no VCs in our family. But old Birch called me up and told me to go down and get his confidential papers out of the chart room. And when I got down there the ship's adjutant, a fellah called Parker was already there.
Ivr: You were down in the chart room?
BS: The chart room, yes. I said to Parker, 'What are you doing.' 'I'm getting the codes, there supposed to be thrown over the side if anything happens.' Lead covering on them. They sink straight away.
Ivr: Where these Admiralty codes?
BS: Yes. Well I said, 'You better carry on. Bring them up to him.'

William Sweeney and a lamp trimmer called Antony launched a small lifeboat on the starboard side but had difficulty letting go some ropes. (The following is taken from the tapes.)

BS: But then fireman Campbell just came up at the engine room stoke hole. I called to him, 'Have you got a knife.' So he, pulling up his little monkey jacket you know, and the next thing she got a second one. Says I, 'To hell.' I looked up and saw the foremast cracking down and I saw the forefunnel ripped out, like in a tem-per. So anyway I slid over the side, it was quite easy because she had a list to port, a good list at this time, so I just slid down along the side.

Ivr: Was discipline good on the ship after you were struck?

BS: Ah, it wasn't really. We had that question of the sergeant and the men he had with them who made it into the midship's lifeboat before she was out of the chocks. And they wouldn't get out. So Jim Carraher, the boson, a great big tall fellah from Wexford, he tried to coax them out. Nothing doing. So he got the military police for them. 'I'm afraid you'll have to do your duty here,' says he. So the MP told the sergeant to get the men out and he didn't seem to understand. The poor fellah was dazed I suppose. Be God he shot him through the head, and they got out then. Course nothing like that was mentioned ... (He continues here to recount other regretful incidences in the lifeboats.)

Ivr: Did you see the ship going down from the lifeboat?

BS: Our lifeboat I suppose drifted around the stern and at this time she was nearly gone. And quite a lot of young Tommies sitting on the rail and I was shouting at them to 'Jump!' And signalling to them to jump because it was the only chance they had getting hold of something. But they just sat there. The mailboats had a very nice, what would you call it?, a crest on the stern. It wasn't just a plain RMS Leinster, it was more like a scroll, a coloured thing. And then you had these lovely bronze propellers. There was a little bit of light from somewhere and caught them you know with a shaft of sunlight. Anyway she finally went under with this hissing sound. The air whished through the propeller shafts I'd imagine.

Ivr: It must have been quite an awesome sight from the lifeboat just under the stern to see her going down?

BS: Ah yes.

Ivr: Tell me what you felt or what she looked like as she went down?

BS: To me, I was only a young lad. I loved ships and I loved the old Leinster. I'd been in her so long. I don't know, a sense of loss. You had lost something, an old friend. Ah it was a great sadness for me.

Ivr: When you were in the boat you were holding the Northumberland soldier. What was the scene like? Were you in sight of land?

BS: No, you couldn't see land at that time either. Nor there was no sign of the destroyer either, for about, it must have been a couple of hours after.

Ivr: Had the ship gone down at that stage?

BS: Oh yes. She went down in ten minutes.

Ivr: How many people were lost?

BS: Ah, very hard to know. I think over 500. I don't think there were 200 saved.

Ivr: How long where you in the lifeboat before the destroyer came?

BS: A whole two hours.

138

Ivr: And what happened when the torpedo struck?

BS: Well Paddy Ryan was telling me a couple of days afterwards that he gave the usual tap on the key and got a reply back. And then immediately, very faintly 'I got this SOS, SOS, SOS, TORPEDOED, TORPEDOED and the name of the ship.' So Paddy broadcasted it, he knew there was something wrong with the Leinster's wireless mast. And he broadcast it immediately. And it was picked up of course all round the place. And two destroyers picked it up too.

Ivr: You mentioned one of the destroyers, the Lively. Which was the other?

BS: The Mallard.

Ivr: And they were on station in the Irish Sea, were they?

BS: Yes, they were attached to the Kingstown Naval Base. And there was a sort of little inquiry in Captain Heuston's room a day or two afterwards. They asked me to go over. Well Admiral Dennison was in charge of the naval base at Kingstown and he said to Paddy Ryan, 'Do you think the *Leinster*'s signals could have been picked up in the harbour at Kingstown.' 'Of course says Paddy.' And says Dennison, 'You mustn't say that.' Apparently they were not keeping a watch on the ships in the harbour.

Ivr: Tell me something about the inquiry, Bill.

BS: They wanted me to tell about it because the whole thing was hushed up.

Ivr: Gavan Duffy was the Judge?

BS: No, Gavan Duffy was appearing for the next of kin. The lady who was drowned, Georgina O'Brien. She lived in Dun Laoghaire. And then you had Denis Henry KC, he appeared for the Company. And then you had Sergeant Hanna, he appeared for the Admiralty. It was held in the courthouse in Kingstown before Mr Rat Lynch. They call it an inquest. But what they were really doing was trying to find out the number of British troops that there were on board. When I was in the courtroom early, Commander Dillon of the Royal Navy, an expert in submarines, nice chap. The next thing he saw me sitting in the courtroom and he called me out. I went out and the policeman stopped me and said that witnesses are not allowed to leave the courtroom once they enter. 'Ah' says Dennison, 'The boy wants to have a smoke he's here too early.' He said to me, 'Take your time before answering and all this will be over soon.' I found out why you took your time.

Ivr: Certain things didn't come out at the inquiry?

BS: O lord yes. Like the number of troops or uniformed personnel. That didn't come out at all.

Ivr: The shooting of the sergeant in the lifeboat?

BS: Oh no. That was never mentioned.

Ivr: Why was that?

BS: Oh God. That would be dreadful. That was all 'kid glove' affair. That was never mentioned at all except the odd view.

Ivr: You mentioned the ships at Kingstown were not keeping watch. Radio watch?

BS: Well that was, they were supposed to keep watch, wireless watch on the submarine chasers. Apparently the British officer was keeping watch in, up in Kingstown and didn't bother.

Ivr: Was that mentioned at the inquiry?

BS: Oh, not a sound.

Bill Sweeney's recollections are remarkably sharp and confirm such facts as the mast not falling until the second torpedo struck, the faint radio message, the regrettable incidents in getting out the lifeboats and the undue delay by the Admiralty in reaching the scene. A little curious is his total and accurate recollection of all of the KCs and witnesses, but he gave the name of Mr Rat Lynch to the official presiding over the inquest and not Mr Rafferty as was reported. He also confirms that certain aspects of the incident were hushed up, not just to deprive the enemy of important strategic information but also to deceive the public for political reasons. His narrative is far more extensive than the items I have included here and is now an important contribution to our folklore.

Irish people have long had the ability to recall disastrous events in song and verse, and here is a suitable ballad collected on the east coast of Ireland and recalled by the people of County Wexford. It was written down by Patrick Doyle, Kilmacoe, on 26 August, 1946. The words are included in the excellent and charming publication *Songs of the Wexford Coast*.

The Mail Boat, Leinster

You feeling hearted Christians all in country or in town,
Come listen to my doleful song which I have just penned down.
'Tis all about that German act, that awful tragedy,
When the Dublin Mail Boat Leinster was sunk in the Irish Sea.

On the tenth day of October, Nineteen eighteen, the year,
This Mail Boat on her passage went, I mean to let you hear,
With six hundred and ninety passengers and seventy of a crew,
She sailed away from Kingstown Quay and for Holyhead bound to.

In pride and stately grandeur did the Leinster plough her way,
And all on board were of good cheer with spirits light and gay;
Not fearing that the U-boat lay hid beneath the wave,
That would send them soon unto their doom, and give a watery grave.

The German monster came on them when they did least expect,
And fired torpedoes at the boat, which quickly took effect.
Her boilers burst; the flames ascend with fury to the sky;
Mid the echo of the deafening dim you could hear the women cry.

Oh, the Leinster now is sinking fast; she's going down by the head,
And many, too, while in their bunks are numbered with the dead.
The passengers, their life belts on, unto the boats repair,
While cries for help do rend the skies in sad and wild despair.

Now to conclude and finish-my doleful lines to close;
May the Lord have mercy on their souls and grant them sweet repose.
Beside the Mail Boat, Leinster, they quietly now do sleep,
In the cold and changeless waters of the Irish Sea so deep.

In conclusion

However frequent and misguided wars may seem to be, it is always the young who are called in great numbers to lay down their lives for the cause. It has not always been for the noblest of reasons but, then again, in cases it may have been ultimately necessary to free a nation or a continent from a cruel dictator. In any event, these young servicemen and women who may not have been on the battlefield com-pletely voluntarily, endured unthinkable injuries and hardships and often performed great and repeated feats of heroism. They accomplished all this whilst far from their kin and homeland in order to grant and protect the freedoms which we enjoy today. Let us remember the lost youth who never lived to share our good fortune.

Appendix 1

The following is a list of those military personnel who were lost as a result of the attack on the *Leinster* and were buried at Grangegorman Military Cemetery, Blackhorse Avenue, Dublin. The list includes military personnel buried there up to the last day of October 1918.

Adams, G. Private. Lancashire Reg: Adey, W. Lieutenant. Cambrian Yeomanry: Alderidge, Corporal. RAF: Aldworthy, D. Lieutenant. Royal Berkshire: Alexander, K. KOJB: Andrews, G. Sergeant. 6th Canadian: Argent, E. Private. Wiltshire Yeomanry: Auty, F. Private. East Riding Reg: Baker, A. London Yeomanry: Bakley, J. Private. Dorset Yeomanry: Ball, T. Private. Yorkshire Hussars: Barclay, D. Lieutenant. Lancashire Hussars: Bardon. Private. Australian Forces: Barnes. Private. 48th Batallion Australian JF: Barraclough, J. Private. Royal Defence Corps: Barradell, E. Private. East Riding Reg: Bauers, F (J). Private. Yorkshire Hussars: Bennison, W. Private. 12th Lancers: Bernard, T. Private. RAM Corps: Billings, C. Corporal. MFPO: Birch, J. (F) Private. Lancashire Hussars Yeomanry: Bishop. Private. Scottish Horse Reg: Black, J. (F) Corporal. West Cambrian Yeomanry: Blackhurst. Royal Defence Corps: Boon, C. Private. Essex Cyclist: Boughey. Lieutenant. Rifle Brigade: Bowen, R. Private. Lancashire Hussars: Bradley, W. Private. RAO Corps: Brassington, A. Sergeant. 3rd Lincolns: Brennan, J. Sergeant. Welsh Fusiliers: Bryant, C. Private. City of London Yeomanry: Bugg, E. Private. East Riding Yeomanry: Burnes, D. Captain. R.A.m. Corps: Burns. Private. Canadian Artillery Brigade: Butt, E. Driver. AF Corps: Cahill. Gunner. RF Artillery: Campbell, GRC Lt Commander (and wife Eileen and child Elizabeth Augusta): Carew, E. Sapper. Royal Engineers: Carter, E. Private. 29th Australian JF: Colgate, A. Private. Royal Sussex: Conlon, E. Rec. Leinster Reg: Costello, J. Bdg Royal G Artillery: Crichton. Air Mechanic. RAF: Croley. Private. 4th Reserves: Crompton. Private. LN Lancashire Reg: Cross, R. Private. Scottish Horse: Deane, A. Private. Essex Cyclist: Demaine. Corporal. LNL: Dillingham, W. Private. Scottish Horse Reg: Donnelly, O. Private. Royal Defence Corps: Double, A. Private. LN Lanes: Doyle, H. Lieutenant. New Zealand Forces: Dunne, W. (N) Private. 5th Lancers: Dysart, J. (F) Private. Labour Corps: Eade, A. Sick Attendant. Royal Navy: Eddig, S. Corporal. Welsh Reg: Elphins, F. Private. City of London Yeomanry: Emblein, F. Private. Royal Defence Corps: Evans, L. Private. Worchester Reg: Felton. Boy. Royal Dublin Fusiliers: Finch, W. Corporal. Royal Defence Corps: Fingleton, W. Royal Welsh Fusiliers: Finlen, J. Private. GTTOM Staff. (Canadian): Fishwick. Sergeant. Royal Welsh Fusiliers: Flaherty, M. Private. Irish Guards: Forde, A. GMF. AF Corps: Freeman, E. Sergeant. Essex Yeomanry: Frizlas, P. Corporal. NZASC: Galbraith, A. Private. RAD Corps: Gallivan. Corporal. Royal Irish Reg: Gilligan, P. Private. RAF: Gilmore, R. Corporal. Royal Engineers: Grattan, G. Sergeant. 4th Australian: Gwyn, D. Lieutenant. Canadian Dragoons: Hall, W. Lieutenant. Lancashire Reg: Hampton, A. Private. 3rd KL: Harlwood, F. (J) Private. 21st Lancashire: Harvey. Private. WG Wiltshire Reg: Hayes, B. Lieutenant. Royal Berkshire: Hayes, E. Gunner. RSA: Henderson, R. Private. Royal Defence Corps:

Hewitt, L. Private. Royal Defence Corps: Higgins, J. Pts. 200th Manatoba: Hill, G. Private. Royal Defence Corps: Hiscock, T. Private. Wiltshire Yeomanry: Horner, A. Private. City of London Yeomanry: Hough. F. Seaman. Royal Navy: Howard, P. Corporal. King's Liverpool Reg: Hullay, F. CFM Yorkshire Hussars: Hunt, G. Private. East Riding Yeomanry: Hustwick. Private. Yorkshire Hussars: Kehurst, E. Private. Scottish Horse Reg: Lalton, W. London Yeomanry: Lament, A. Lieutenant. King's Liverpool Reg: Laws, W. Private. City of London: Leather. Petty officer. Royal Navy: Leatherland, R. Lieutenant. AF Corps: Lee. Private. King's Liverpool Reg: Lundy, J. Corporal. Royal Welsh Fusiliers: Lynch, G. Private. Royal Dublin Fusiliers: Marsh, C. Private. RAM Corps: Mccabe. Driver. R. Fart: Mccauley, T. Corporal. RAMC: Mcdonnell, T. Private. Machine Gun Corps: Mcintosh, F. Royal Welsh Fusiliers: Mckellard, D. CGMJ Somerset Yeomanry: Mclean. Sergeant. 3rd. KFLI: Megroft, F. Sergeant. RAO Corps: Monahan, T. Driver. RFA: Moone, S. Private. City of London Yeomanry: Moore, R. Private. Wiltshire Yeomanry: Mosse, O. Colonel. RM Fusiliers (and wife Mrs E.): Mullholland, W. Private. Yorkshire Hussars: O'Connor, M. Corporal. CEC: O'Halloran, A. Private. RAMC: Pendleton, J. Private. Irish Guards: Pilgrim, A. Chief Petty Officer. Royal Navy: Pomfret, A. Private. Sussex Cyclist: Power, P. Private. West Cumbrian Yeomanry: Pritchwood, W. Private. Sussex Cyclist: Probert, J. (F) Private. Labour Corps: Prosser, F. RFM. RS Artillery: Quin, Q. Private. King's Lancers: Quinly, H. Private. FI Horse: Rayner, G. Private. Lancashire Hussars: Reilly, T. Private. RAF: Robinson, J. Sergeant. Black Watch: Roche. Private. R. M. Fusiliers: Rose, J. Sergeant. Base Section. USA: Smith, D. Private. Cameron Highlanders: Smith, J. Private. Labour Corps: Smith, M. Private. Australian Forces. (13th Co. 19th Bat.): Spurges. Private. Wiltshire Reg: Standing, W. Private. Essex Reg: Stephens. Private. East Riding Yeomanry: Thomas, F. (J) Sergeant. King's Liverpool Reg: Thomas, E. Private. Royal Welsh Fusiliers: Thompson, A. Private. RAM Corps: Thompson, R. Driver. RF Artillery: Unknown soldier: Unknown soldier: Unsworth, J. Sergeant. King's Lancers: Walker, G. Corporal. Lancashire Yeomanry: Walker, T. Private. Royal Defence Corps: Wallis, G. Lieutenant. Wiltshire Reg: Watkins, F. Sapper. Wats. Private. KLL fn(?): Wells, R. Corporal. 14th Suffolk: Westwell, A. Miss. QMAAC (buried in officer's plot): Whittaker, G. Sergeant. Royal Defence Corps: Whittlan, C. Private. Royal Engineers Yorkshire: Wilcox, s. Sergeant. Police: Wilkes, P. and wife. Lieutenant. AF Corps: Williams, J. Corporal. Royal Defence Corps: Winterbourne, F. Captain. London Regiment: Wood, G. Corporal. 21st Hussars: Woodgate, J. (F) Private. Royal Depot RAF: Woods, J. Private. Labour Corps:

The above list is inclusive from the date of the disaster until the end of October, 1918. Although there are many more military deaths recorded thereafter it was impossible without extensive research to determine which were a result of the sinking of the Leinster. There are also many enlisted personnel who were not buried at Grangegorman military cemetery but elsewhere, such as those who were returned to Holyhead and so on. It also does not include a significant number of bodies which were never recovered.

Lost crew members

The following is just a short list of crew members who lived locally at Kingstown but were sadly lost aboard the Leinster:

Smith, Seaman, Desmond Ave
H. Longmore, Seaman, Mulgrave St
W.J. Brennan, Seaman, Lr George's St.,
Brown, Fireman, Sallynoggin
B. Murphy, Fireman, Glasthule
M. Harvey, Fireman, Kingstown
Cody, Fireman, Kingstown
P. Loughlin, Fireman, Kingstown
H. Tyrell, Quartermaster, Janesville
D. Whelan, Quartermaster, Kingstown
Kehoe, Crewman, Eden Tce
Hickey, Greaser, Tivolli Tce
Arthur J. Jeffries, Wireless operator, Gleageary.

Not a member of the crew, but deserving a special mention owing to the irony of the earlier loss of her husband from the local Kingstown lifeboat when it attended the shipwrecked *Palme* in the Bay, and the ultimate death of her dear daughter to whom she was travelling to be with, was Mrs Saunders of York Road, Kingstown.
    May they all rest in peace.

It is easy to forget that the channel crossing and its mail boats belonged not only to Kingstown but equally to Holyhead. Many of the crew who sailed in the *Leinster* were from there and we must remember all of the twenty-four crew who hailed from there: R. Antony, Bath St; W. Birch, The Sycamores; R. Hughes, East Lynne; J. Inglis, Newry Fawr; J. Jones, Cecil St; H. Jones, Llainfain; W. Mathias, Newry St; P. Michael, Newry St; W. Nicklin, Park St; H. Owen, Tower Gardens; R. Roberts, London Rd; W. Roberts, Winn St; R. Thomas, Rock St; T. Williams, Hilton Lleich; J. Williams, Gilbert St; R. Williams, Rock St; J. Crispin, Churston; O. Jones, Robert St; W. Lewis, Newry St; E. Moore, Redmond St; Louisa Parry, Fair View; H. Rowlands, Llynwood; G. Williams, Summerhill; R. Williams, George's St. May they too rest in peace.

Sources of research

Great Britain
Cammell Laird, Shipbuilders, Birkenhead.
Department Of Transport, Sunley House, London.
Guildhall Library, London.
Gwynedd County Library, Holyhead, Wales.
Hydrographic Office, MOD, Taunton, Somerset.
Imperial War Museum, Lambeth Road, London.
Llangefni Archives, Holyhead, Wales.
Lloyd's Register of Shipping, London.
Ministry Of Defence, London.
National Maritime Museum, Greenwich.
Naval Historical Library, Empress State Building, London.
Public Records Office, Kew, London.
Royal Airforce Museum, Hendon, London.
Science Museum, South Kensington.
The Salvage Association, London.
The Treasury Solicitor, 28 Broadway, London.
Trinity House Light House Service, London.
Tyne And Wear Archive Services, Newcastle-On-Tyne.
Ulster Folk And Transport Museum, Bangor County Down.
Wirral Museum, Birkenhead.

Republic of Ireland
Marine Research, Ballsbridge Terrace, Ballsbridge, Dublin 4.
Commissioners of Irish Lights, Pembroke Street Lower, Dublin.
Gilbert Library, Pearse Street, Dublin.
Irish Railway Society, Heuston Station, Kingsbridge, Dublin.
Maritime Institute, Dun Laoghaire, Dublin.
Military Archives, Cathal Bruagh Barracks, Rathmines
National Archives, Bishop Street, Dublin.
National Library, Kildare Street, Dublin.
Representative Church Body Library, Braemor Road, Dublin.
State Papers Office, Four Courts, Dublin.
Trinity Library, Trinity College, Dublin.

United States
Department of the Navy, Washington.
National Archives, Washington.
National Historical Centre, Washington.

Germany
Federal German Military Archives, Freiburg.
U-boat Archives, Cuxhaven.

Publications which were referenced

Airship Pilot No. 28. Captain T.B. Williams. (Courtesy of Noel Flanagan, Malahide, Dublin.)
Amazing Adventure E. K.Chatterton, Hurst and Blackett Ltd.
An Phost (Irish postal magazine), December, 1988.
Anglesey and Lleyn Shipwrecks Ian Skidmore.
Ball's History of County Dublin Francis E. Ball, HSP, 1902.
Beating The U-Boats E. K.Chatterton, Rich and Cowan, London, 1936.
British Underwater Sub Aqua Club (magazine), BSAC.
British Vessels Lost at Sea 1914-1918 and 1939-1945 Patrick Stephens.
Charles Parsons Rollo Apleyard.
Danger Zone E.K. Chatterton, Hurst and Blackett Ltd.
Der Handelskrieg Mit U-Booten Admiral Arno Spindler
Der Krieg Zur Zee Admiral Arno Spindler
Dictionary of Disasters at Sea During the Age of Steam Charles Hocking, Lloyds, London 1969.
Exploring the Lusitania Robert Ballard, Madison Press, Toronto, 1995.
Holyhead and the Great War R. E. Roberts.
Indiscretions of a Naval Censor Rear Admiral Sir Douglas Browning.
Irish Passengers Steamship Services (2 Vols.) D.B. McNeil, 1971.
Longmans Chronicle
Modern Irish Trade and Industry E.J. Riordan.
'My Mystery Ships' Gordon Campbell DSO, Hodder and Stoughton,1928.
Nautical Magazine 1918. (Journal)
New Tales of the Submarine War D. Masters, Eyre and Spottiswood, London, 1935.
Outline of Irish Railway History H.C. Casserley.
Sea Breezes (magazine) July 1961.
Seventy Years Young Pamela Hinkson, Collins 1937.
Shipwrecks of the Irish Coast (2 Vols.) Edward Bourke, 1994-98
Slaughter at Sea Alan Coles, R. Hales, London, 1982.
Submarine Peril Admiral Earl Jellicoe, Cassell, London, 1934.
Submarines Antony Preston.
Surrendered Some Naval Secrets A.S. Griffiths, published by the author.
The Big Blockade E.K. Chatterton, Hurst and Blackett Ltd.
The Communications Worker (magazine) Vol. 7, 1996.
The Most Formidable Thing William Jameson.

The Victory at Sea Admiral Sims and Burton J. Hendrick, J. Murray, London, 1920.
Warships Of World War I Ian Allen Ltd.

Newspapers

New York Herald
London Illustrated News
Irish Times
Evening Herald
The Daily Graphic
The Sphere
The Sunday Express (1965)
The Holyhead Chronicle
The Independent
The Times
Freeman's Journal
The Leprecaun
The Independent
London Gazette

Sources of illustrations

Page 9 - Richard Natkiel in *Longman's Gazette:* page 12 - above *Irish Times;* below National Library: page16 Laurence Collection, National Library: page 21 - *A History of the Royal Air Force and the United States Naval Air Services in Ireland 1913-1923* by Karl E. Hayes: page 23 - Public Records Office, Kew: pages 26-7 - National Archives, Dublin: page 28 - National Archives, Dublin: page 18 - Tom's Directory and author photo: pages 34-7 - Wirral Museum, Birkenhead: page 38 - Maritime Institute, Dun Laoghaire: page 43 Sea Breezes: page 46 - National Library: page 48 - top: Daily Graphic, middle: Sea Breezes, bottom: author: page 50 - Imperial War Museum: page 57 - Laurence Collection, National Library: page 58 - top: National Library, bottom: Noel Brian: page 59 - Noel Brian: page 65 - Imperial War Museum: page 67 - Imperial War Museum: page 68 - courtesy of PPL: page 69 - U-Boat Archives, Cuxhaven: page 75 - U-boat records, National Archives, Washington: page 77 - National Archives, Washington: page 82 - U-Boat Archives, Cuxhaven: page 87 - Mr Crangle: page 89 - National Archives, Washington: page 99 - The Sphere: page 106 - author's compilation from Public Records Office, Kew: page 110 - The Sphere: page 113 - The Sunday Express: page 119 - National Library, Ireland: page 137 - *The Daily Graphic* and author. Other illustrations are the work of the author or are acknowledged in the caption.

The publishers and author have made strenuous attempts to obtain necessary permission for copyright material, yet some owners we have been unable to trace. If they would contact us, we shall be pleased to acknowledge them in any further edition.

INDEX